DESTINED
FOR GREATNESS

LIVING AN INSPIRED LIFE,
FROM HEAD TO TIPPI TOES

SARAH LOWERY NUSE

Destined for Greatness

ISBN: 9798668600250

© 2020 Sarah Nuse

Photography: Bethany Rogers, Hey World Creative
www.heyworldcreative.com

Illustrations: Alaina McGraw, Good Brain Creative Group, LLC

Scripture quotations are taken from the Holy Bible, New International Version®, NIV®. Copyright © 1973, 1978, 1984, 2011 by Biblica, Inc.®.

John Rampton, "25 Reasons Why Hiring Your Relatives Is an Even Worse Idea Than You Suspected," Entrepreneur, July 7, 2017, https://www.entrepreneur.com/article/296592

To all the dreamers, especially my favorite four:

Adam, Lucy, Lola, and Hank

Contents

Foreword

by Bob Goff

If you know Sarah Nuse -- and, since you're holding her book, you're about to -- it won't surprise you to hear she wore a hot pink shirt and a huge smile when I first met her. Ever the dedicated learner, she fiercely took notes between smiles as I spoke to her and thirty other eager dreamers who'd come to my hometown to lean into their dreams. The goal of my Dream Big course is to dive deeper into the just-can't-shake-them ideas people have and start probing them to move forward. My very first conference was held in San Diego in late March of 2017, and I could tell Sarah, for one, was ready for something more.

As she and I sat and talked one-on-one, it was clear to me what she needed to do: she needed to write a book. The depth of her dreams and the progress she had already made by building a business, skillfully speaking to large audiences, and hosting her Destined for Greatness podcast, the next step seemed natural.

"I see a book inside of you," I told her, leaning forward in hopes she would grasp my earnestness. "The world needs to hear your voice."

She smiled and told me the many reasons this wouldn't work. "Bob, I'm not a writer." I have been convinced of many false narratives in my life, too, stories about who I am and what I'm capable of that simply are not true. I have learned when people are negative, they often are using these same limiting beliefs on themselves and casting shadows on others. But Sarah isn't one to sit there and let those limiting beliefs wash over her. If you ever have the opportunity to hear Sarah at one of her many public speaking engagements, you're in for a treat. She so eloquently and energetically shares her story about steeling herself to merge her passion with others' needs to generate purpose. When she speaks to large audiences, your seatmates melt away and you feel she's talking directly to *you*, making your dreams feel within reach. You'll leave empowered and accountable for bringing your ideas to life. Be good every day, she says, and make wise choices; the sky's the limit.

Sarah is the epitome of a big dreamer. Dreaming big is exciting, fun, and a way we lean into all God has planned for our life. Once I convinced Sarah that she had more to say and people who wanted to hear it, she did what she always does, what she's done for decades as a person, a business owner, and a parent: she jumped in with both feet. Over the next six months, Sarah and I had many conversations about what this book would look like. I would often pop up to ask how her writing was going, and she'd share the progress, full of optimism and the focused drive that has made Tippi Toes the major success it is. I believe our role as friends is to encourage one another to keep going, to put one foot in front of the other and *move*. Here's where I insert a joke about how Sarah knows better than anyone the importance of incorporating movement into one's life; see "Tippi Toes."

Another thing Sarah knows better than most? The importance of defining her goals, one of which is to share Jesus with as many people as possible. Her faith turns her inward to examine how to employ her talents to connect others with Him. Many times, Sarah and I talked about her "why." Why do you want to continue growing your business, speaking, podcasting, and so on? When we know *why*, we're given the wheels to take off on our ambition. When we are attached to our why, very little can lead us astray. Once Sarah really allowed her why to lead her, the writing poured out inspired and natural. To be truly, deeply motivated in your life's purpose allows you to jump full steam ahead to what God called you to do. You're better equipped to push away doubt because you know you are called to something greater. Having a strong connection to your purpose is imperative when the days get hard and your vision clouds over. Returning to your belief in your goal and dream emboldens your push. Through Sarah's story, we read how there are several detours in building her business. As a reader, the detours could look very career- and self-defining, but not for our Sarah. Her perseverance and pure passion for her cause encouraged her to dig deeper, and when one road was blocked, wouldn't you know it, she found a new road to explore and push closer to her dream. In some cases, she suited up and constructed that road herself.

What could it be for you? What is your why? Is it big enough to make you move forward in your dream, ever trying, ever reaching for more? I challenge you to read this book and uncover the steps Sarah has taken throughout her life to move forward, despite others' negativity, despite self-doubt, despite her grades. Every story, situation, and even failure has led her to this point. The same is true for you. As you grow, lean in to your passions. Embrace it. You, too, will find that you are, like Sarah says, destined for greatness.

CHAPTER 1

GETTING FIRED

Sometimes the rearview mirror sets the course for our

future.

I wanted a new car like a shark is attracted to blood. My desire was primal. At 18 years old, a new set of wheels was all I thought about. The car I was driving still had that new car smell, you know the one that when you drive off the lot you promise yourself you'll never eat, drink, or breathe in it, just so it keeps that good smell. But that car, the one my parents bought, wasn't actually mine, though I didn't get the message until I was headed off to college. In fact, I had already stuffed my current car, a Toyota RAV4, with college essentials: bath towels, a laundry basket, and, of course, a boom box with the Dixie Chicks on repeat. It was 1999, after all. With a newly opened Dr Pepper can in my cup holder and a handful of sweeTARTS in my lap, I was ready to hit the open road on my way to start freshman year.

My key turned in the ignition when I noticed my mom in the rearview mirror, waving at me to wait. I leaned out of the driver's side window while she delivered the news to my horrified face: I was about to be stranded two hours away, at the University of Oklahoma, without a car.

Dad removed my entire dorm room, one appliance at a time, from the back seat. First, my precious mini fridge, then the toaster. There went the laundry basket and, yes, my boom box. Once my possessions lined the sidewalk, Dad stepped back onto our front lawn, wiping his brow in Oklahoma's August heat. Gloating, my younger sister Megan pulled the car keys out of my hands, the proud *sole* owner now of our RAV4. I helped Dad shove the last overcrowded layer of my life into his car, including my bulletin board neatly pinned with family photos. I averted my eyes from the one of me holding up the car keys on the day we drove it off the lot. How young I was back then. How naive.

My parents and I pulled off, with me in the backseat crying softly at the misunderstanding. That's how we are at 18, right? Caught up in our world of ME. My 16-year-old sister was keeping our car, and I would need to buy one on my own. I caught a glimpse of Megan and our RAV4 in the driveway, getting smaller and smaller as we turned onto 59th Street. What I didn't realize at the time was that it took leaving my perceived gateway to freedom in the rearview mirror to arrest my attention. God knew what a car could do for a girl like me, someone ready to say yes to any adventure. The RAV4 had the room to squeeze five of my best friends together to blow into our high school basketball game. It helped me make it to school on time, shuttled me on hot summer days to sample every snow cone stand in Tulsa. That car, my first, signified freedom, and it was unimaginable to part from. RIP RAV4 -- for me, anyway.

College days are customarily filled with new faces and lasting friendships, and my story doesn't differ. In the middle of the University of Oklahoma's quad, among the sunbathers and the Frisbee club members, I met a girl with a bleach blonde pixie haircut. Her name was Chanda, and we were meant to be best friends, despite my totally judging her at the first impression. I mean, she was the epitome of a small-town girl, and her daily glaring leopard print uniform proved it. But she looked about as thrilled as I did to be rushing for a sorority, so we at least had that much in common. My older sister Jennie was a junior in college and loved sorority life. In going Greek, she met her best friends, participated in special college activities, and, yes, even met some cute boys at "date parties." Plus, I was told that's simply what you *do* when you go to the University of Oklahoma: you rush. As little sisters often do, I blindly followed in her footsteps, wanting, as ever, to be just like Jennie. Yet if the path to making your best friends for life meant standing in the blazing sun, sandals rubbing blisters into your feet while plastering on a fake smile for each sorority house, Chanda and I quickly determined we were not interested. But we were already in too deep, so together we decided to embrace the journey. We instantly bonded, both homesick and a bit lonely, and together we begrudgingly pledged Kappa Alpha Theta. First impressions are often wrong, and here was the lesson for me on not one but two accounts: Chanda and sorority life. Both turned out to be amazing parts of my life, but I'd be remiss if I didn't let you in on this next piece of information: I couldn't have known at the time, but this collaborative, supportive friendship would give me the confidence to start the most rewarding career I ever could have imagined, all while still in college. In 2 Corinthians 12:9, God says, "My grace is sufficient for you." Before I was knitted in my mother's womb, before my parents decided to send me off to college without a car, before playlists were invented, God had a plan. Just then, as Chanda and I connected, it was like pressing the play button on my old boom box. The music to my life began.

Chanda had a car, but don't start judging me; we would have been best friends regardless. Looking back at how God gave me just enough, I have to laugh, because Chanda's car barely ran. If we look at the phrase "just enough," it means not too much and not too little. Just. Enough.

It ran: just enough.

The locks worked: just enough.

The radio played tunes: just enough.

The driver's side door ... didn't open at all. But the passenger's side did! So my friend and I crawled in one at a time and started up the red jalopy she referred to as "The Piece," and did what two girls in college do with a set of wheels. For a short amount of time, it was just enough. Until it wasn't. It became not enough for me to crawl into the passenger's side of my best friend's ride. It wasn't enough to track Chanda down across campus every time I needed to borrow The Piece's keys once again. I needed more: my own freedom, independence, autonomy. This outgoing social butterfly felt held back without her wings -- er, wheels. God created that spirit within me. He doled out His grace as needed, His idea of portion control, calling out of us patience and perseverance. I knew I needed my own car, so the time had come to find a job.

It was October, and Chanda thought the idea of a job sounded fun. The extra money would, in fact, help pay the gas bill for her to trot off to the other state college to visit her boyfriend Matt. So as new adults in our adult relationships, money was *imperative*. We jumped into The Piece -- or, rather, crawled through the passenger's side one at a time, donning our new Kappa Alpha Theta t-shirts, running shorts, and tennis shoes: the uniform of sorority sisters across campus. After filling out fifteen restaurant job applications in Norman, Oklahoma, we made one last stop. (It might have been all that Chanda's car could have handled.) We parked

The Piece at On The Border Mexican Grill & Cantina. The smell of grease and fajitas filled the air, our shoes squeaked against the sticky black floor, and the building was desolate in the afternoon light. A man I considered old at the time -- gosh, at least *30*-- met us with curiosity as he appraised these two ill-dressed girls applying for jobs. On Jeff's ugly purple shirt, I spotted the word we'd been encountering all day: manager. Taking his position of authority, Jeff inquired about the significance of looking for a job in the middle of the semester instead of securing one in August, like all the other students. *Awfully disapproving for someone with the hair of Elmer Fudd*, I thought. But nevermind that, because he quickly found out we had little to no experience serving customers, although Chanda had filled fountain drinks and flipped burgers at The Big T, the only restaurant for miles in her hometown of Thomas, Oklahoma. Unexcited but without options, our friendly smiles and desperation were enough to get us hired.

We each worked twenty hours a week at OTB, as we liked to call it, while maintaining fifteen hours of our college course load. School was a complete disaster for me. I got into the university on probation, meaning my high school grades weren't actually good enough to land me there. Thankfully, the University offered grace, and let me in with the understanding I would improve my academics. Probation is where I stayed semester after semester. I didn't wrestle to get an A, rather a C, and barely. If shirts with sayings on them were cool back then, I would have rocked one that said "Cs are the bee's knees." Or "Cs, please." Or better yet, "Cs for my keys." Jokes aside, I felt confined in school. Brimming with ideas and this supernatural need to make my own income, I did what I needed to do to earn a C and focused the largest part of my energy on something more tangible. It would be years before I understood this as "maximizing focus."

I'd had a desire to work since I started teaching dance for neighborhood kids in my front yard at the age of twelve. It didn't stop there: in high school between classes and sports practices, I taught ballet, tap, and jazz at Miss Shelly's School of Dance, babysat for the Mandeville family on weekends, and helped my mom at the weekend birthday parties she threw. (My mom, one of the first entrepreneurs I knew. She rented Miss

Shelly's studio on the weekend and hosted little kids' parties. Dances, games, music, and cake were included. Her small idea took off, and before she knew it, she was booked for four parties a weekend. When I could, I would help!) This need to stay busy remained with me through college. You name it, I did it. I gave out samples of chili at monster truck rallies for Wolf Brand Chili. I had a headset and a section in Wal-Mart, where I taught shoppers how to use the new Swiffer mop. I was even spotted in Walgreens encouraging customers to feel the difference between Kleenex with lotion compared to regular tissue. As quickly as I made my money, I spent it, too. I wasn't a stranger to cute new outfits, lunches out with my friends, or anything else that seemed to be a college girl's necessity at the time.

Trying to balance work and school meant becoming self-disciplined because I knew if my grades suffered, I wouldn't be able to keep that job. College was never an option for me; it was a *must*. I put the pressure on myself, and my parents didn't waiver, either. It was what was expected. At the time, I had a deep desire to be an elementary school teacher, and college was the way to achieve this goal. I am thankful I did, because it was here in the juggling jobs with school where I really found myself and my way. The effort I applied to my schoolwork, trying to learn and produce anything better than a C, can only be described as rigorous. Like a drill instructor who expects excellence from his soldiers -- shoes polished and shirts pressed -- I arrived to class on time, studied, and never skipped class. Even if I tried my hardest, which was all the time, I still produced Cs. I was like an ant shouldering the largest crumb up a steep incline. Like that ant, my focus never wavered. One grueling step at a time, no matter how heavy my course workload, or my heart.

My freshman year ended with a new slogan I gave myself: Cs get degrees. I was still a few thousand dollars short for a down payment on a car. Had I saved my money as diligently as I showed up for work, I might have had enough for a car, but that was yet another lesson learned. As the year ended, I needed a little break from refilling sodas and flipping tortillas. Growing up, going to our local theater Discoveryland was my family's annual summer tradition. We'd watch the Rodgers and Hammerstein play *Oklahoma* outdoors under the stars, with live horses and loud shotguns onstage. I decided to audition to be a territory dancer, which was part ballet, some partner dancing, and a little bit of acting all wrapped up in one. Tryouts were slated for the end of April, so I hitched a ride home that weekend for my audition and to get in some family time. I was number 213 in the tryouts, out of close to 400 hopefuls. There were only eight positions given to territory dancers, so I was optimistic but not overconfident.

I sat outside the hotel lobby waiting for my number to be called to enter the ballroom. For an hour, we would learn six different routines. At the end of the hour, we were asked to perform with our group in front of a table of five judges. Pen and paper in hand, they watched us auditioning, then glanced down at their papers to write fierce notes. The judges didn't offer a lot of smiles; rather, they studied every step and misstep we dancers made. I had failed in past auditions and been mortified to share the news, so I went the cool-as-a-cucumber route while waiting to hear back from Discoveryland and acted like I was still keeping my summer plans open. I didn't want to let on to family and friends that I longed for this position. I mean, what if I didn't make it? "Failure" wasn't a word I wanted attached to me. I limited who I told about the tryouts and waited patiently for a few weeks. If I made the show, the director would send me a letter at my parents' address in early May.

Mid-May came, and I hadn't heard a word. I sat on the floor of my dorm room amid half-packed suitcases making a list of different places I could work over the summer. The day I was set to move back home, my mom walked into my dorm room with a letter in her hand. The return address: Discoveryland. I was one of the eight dancers chosen to dance six nights a week in front of a crowd of 500. My hours were 4 p.m. to 11 p.m. and my start date was three days from now, but no matter the quick turnaround: I was ecstatic.

For two weeks, we rehearsed from 8 a.m. to 6 p.m. and opened the show Memorial Day weekend. The summer was filled with new friendships, late nights, lots of dancing, and, yes, saving money! How thankful I was to live at home while working. The show came to a close, and thanks to getting paid for this dancing gig, I'd made just enough for a down payment in just enough time to buy a car before my sophomore year. My parents took me to a local dealership, where I spotted a 1994 Toyota Celica. The five-speed, cherry red ragtop sat facing the street with its top down. I didn't even care about the heavy perfume scent left by the previous owner because *I* was about to be the new owner, and a proud one at that. I couldn't have been more excited. We sat on stiff leather seats across from the loan officer, who explained what the monthly payments would look like. I nodded my head and happily signed every signature spot. My heart burst with pride as my hand gripped the keys. I'd earned this car, and the feeling of doing it on my own would stay with me the rest of my life. Every taco delivered, every time I wore my ugly On The Border uniform and orthopedic-looking shoes to class made this day possible. The late nights dancing at the theater despite blisters from dancing in heels that pounded against the concrete night after night. It was all worth it. Now that I had taken care of the down payment, I would just need to continue waitressing to cover my monthly payments of $234 -- quite a bit of money for a college student! Without delay, I cruised around Tulsa with the top down, letting my hair breeze in the warm summer air. My first stop: pick up my friend Kathleen to show her my new set of wheels. I felt proud that I had worked hard for this car, and maybe also a little prideful that I was the only girl in my friend group who knew how to drive a five-speed. This meant no sharing with my sisters, which made me smile all the bigger. At the end of the summer, I stuffed my new car full of those college necessities my dad had unloaded from the family RAV4 the year before and headed back to Norman. I was most excited to see Chanda because she knew well my big goal of purchasing my own car. I can only imagine she had a sense of relief at not having to share The Piece. This time, I would be the one letting her drive my car.

It was a couple of months into the school year. The air was crisp, the first indication of football season in Oklahoma. To know me is to know two things: I love Jesus, and I love football. If you are a football fan, you know Oklahoma football can be very exciting. One of my closest high school friends, Caroline, was now a student at Notre Dame, and we were set to play them that season! I eagerly bought football game tickets for my sister and myself without a thought of what my work schedule might look like that day. The week before the game, I clocked in at On The Border and casually threw out my exciting football news to my co-workers. In my elated state, I didn't understand my boss's warning about losing my job if I didn't show up to work that weekend. Living in Sooners territory, I assumed he would understand just how exciting it would be to have tickets to this particular game. Instead, he issued an ultimatum.

"Sarah, if you don't come to work, you won't have a job," Jeff said plainly.

I was so excited about my trip that my conversation with my boss faded fast from my mind. Surely I'd still have a job after the game. After all, I needed $234 to pay for my beloved car that month. Didn't Jeff understand that? I packed my bags, met up with my sister Megan, who was a junior in high school, and climbed aboard the bus that would take us the twelve hours up to Notre Dame. When I think back to that weekend, Megan and I had the time of our lives hanging out with our friends and thoroughly enjoying the experience of cheering on our team. But the game didn't go our way, so after Oklahoma lost to Notre Dame, we headed back home, still reflecting on the great weekend despite our team's defeat.

When I went into work to see where I was on the schedule for the upcoming week, I oddly couldn't find my name. I prodded my co-workers but received awkward answers in return. Still unaware I'd been fired, I found my boss in his usual purple shirt, hunched over his office computer. He did not look happy to see me. I asked why I had been left off the schedule. He spoke matter-of-factly, reiterating his ultimatum about missing work for the football game -- except this time, it started to make sense. Sheepishly, I asked him if I was fired. The answer was yes.

Losing my job completely crushed me. But just as quickly as my employment ended, my sadness turned to real panic. Remember, I had just bought a car in August, and now it was October, and I had a $234 car payment due November 1. As a young college student, my first thought was to call my parents. I dialed their number and quickly explained my dire situation.

"Mom, Dad, I got fired," I said. "I need some money."

Instead of bailing me out and giving me money, my parents gave me a brilliant idea, one that would launch a lucrative career and take me from Oklahoma to California to standing in front of Mark Cuban on *Shark*

Tank. Never would I have thought that I would be running a company with franchises around the world, but this humbling moment pushed me to become a better worker, leader, and innovator. Mom reminded me of the days I spent dancing as a student at Miss Shelly's School of Dance and the summers I in turn taught neighborhood children to dance. After a week of coordinating little bodies in unison, the kids would perform for their parents in my front yard back then. At 12 years old, running my own dance camp wasn't a bad business idea. I charged each student $10 for the week of classes, training them for three hours a day. Looking back now, my mom was a saint to not only let me do this, but to encourage me the entire time as well. She recognized my young entrepreneurialism, and her encouragement allowed me to dream big, even while in middle school. The first summer, I taught five little dancers, but I continued hosting this summer camp every year until I left for college. Each year it grew. With the success of my dance school under my belt, I teamed up with my athletic friend Caroline to offer a combination dance and basketball camp during our summers off from high school.

When my mom reminded me about this camp experience, I realized I could recreate it while attending the university. Quickly running out of money and desperate to make my car payment, I drove to the closest daycare center. I didn't have any paperwork, a plan, or even a name for my business. All I had was an idea and hope. Remember that determination that won me the waitress job? It's the same characteristic that also landed me my first daycare dancing gig.

"Hi, I'm Sarah. I would like to come teach dance to your kids." That was my entire pitch to the daycare's directors. It was clear by the delighted looks on their faces that my determination and desperation were palpable. Hired. When asked the name of my business, I responded like I did to my own name.

"Tippi Toes," I immediately answered with confidence. And nothing felt more natural. That exact moment, in Norman, Oklahoma, my business was born. And not only was a business born, but an entrepreneur -- though my mom could attest I'd long been a businessperson. What dancing does in my life is similar to what music does for a movie: it synchronizes everything to a point, a climax, when sometimes everyone but the main character knows what is so obvious. But in my case, it had always been so clear to me. Dancing was the theme to my life. You see, sometimes when we are in the moment of getting out of a mess, we think small, when really there is an adventure so much bigger and better waiting for us. Technically, for this month, I was halfway to my car payment with the work I'd already done at OTB. I had five little dancers who were going to dance with me that first month. This was enough to at least get started, but I knew I'd have to make more headway later. All I was focused on, though, was making that payment *this* month.

When I enrolled in college, I went in thinking I would be a schoolteacher, but the class Introduction to Elementary Math was the course that killed me: I literally failed it. (More on that later.) I needed to declare a major, but it was so hard when there were so many possibilities. I loved kids, so teaching made sense. I loved taking care of people, so for three days I changed my major to nursing until I realized how much I hated being around sick people: a prerequisite for the job. I knew in my heart I would succeed at whatever I put my mind to, but there wasn't a major that matched my heart. Starting Tippi Toes gave me an adrenaline rush. I was doing what I loved -- teaching kids dance -- and it was the first time while being at school I felt I was actually good at something, and the money my students' parents paid me seemed to confirm it. The more I taught, the more kids would sign up. The more kids who signed up, the more money I made. The more money I made, I could not only pay my car payment but I could also afford so much more. It was self-sufficiency, and I loved every single minute of it.

Time and again, people ask how I did it. My answer: I was desperate. (Cue the song "Desperado.") There I was sweating out that car payment, just praying this hatched plan would work. God, as he always does, one-upped me and set the path for this company that continues to grow right before my very eyes. As I leaned in and grew as a businesswoman, I learned these five steps that always got me to my next goal, without fail.

1. **Write it down!** If we don't see it, we don't know it. When we write it, we remember it. It sticks to us like chewed gum on the bottom of a shoe. We're held accountable, and our goals are less scary. It

is essential to see our goals on paper. Write it, then read it out loud and believe you can make it happen!

2.   **Develop the purpose.** Know the small and big reasons you're driven to reach your goals. They can be silly, impactful, irrelevant to others, but they must be important to *you*. That pressing, that burning in the heart isn't indigestion. It isn't just your mind playing games on you; it's God calling out the greatness inside each one of us. He has called us for bigger, more, and we must be obedient to that call in our life.

3.   **Face the fear.** That devil, he thinks he can have his way, but I say look him in the face the minute you hear his words in your ears. He is not worth it, and all fear does is waste our time, like scrolling through social media while waiting in the carpool line. Don't give fear a voice in your head; punish it like a criminal who just got the death penalty, lock it away, and never let it see the light of day.

4.   **Set the clock.** It's go time. We dream about it and talk about it. Now it's time to do it. Movement on a goal begins to rapidly unfold our dreams. I like

to think of what my end goal is and then work backward. Think big and then break down the steps you must do to get there in small daily deposits. What can I do in one day, what can I do in one week, what can I do in one month? Put dates next to each task. I like to make my dates uncomfortable to push me along faster. If I think a task should be completed in a week, I give it a date of three days out to push me to do it. These steps allow us to have daily bite-size tasks, and we see substantial growth when we are consistent.

5. **Celebrate small victories.** Day in and day out, we can find the reasons why we are working hard. These small victories, these nuggets, are what keep us going. They're instant gratification, and it's enough to take us to the next nugget and the next until the end goal is in sight. It could look like an email back from a potential client, it could be a graphic you had been waiting on, or a product that you are finally holding in your hand. It might be a new sentence in the book you're writing, a down payment on a building, a signed contract, or even simply a conversation that sparks an idea.

We inch closer to the very thing we want the most and share our small wins with those who are cheering for us on our journey.

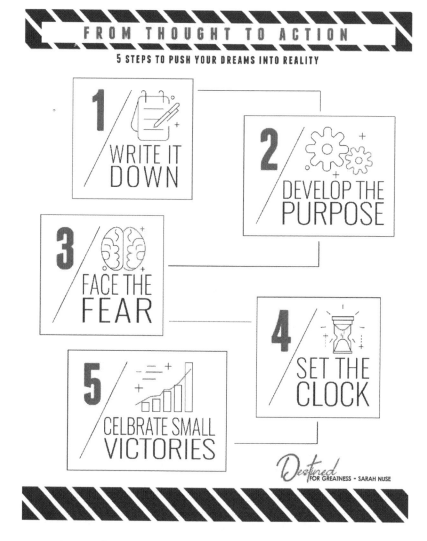

When I first wrote down my goals and dreams early in 2002, it came out to three pages. What I quickly realized was I was spread too thin. There was no way I could accomplish becoming a competitive swimmer (if you know me, this is laughable), learning Spanish, and starting a Mary Kay business while also going to school full-time and picking up every odd job that slightly sounded fun. When I shrunk my initial list down and became focused on just four goals, they suddenly appeared manageable. As Tippi Toes began to take shape, my first four goals looked like this:

1. Teach 50 students per week (At the time, I had 20 children dancing.)

2. Pay my car payment each month

3. Learn to sew costumes

4. Find more schools to bring Tippi Toes to

This has been the key in my everyday life: do less with more focus. Because, you see, God instilled in me a spirit of power, not a spirit of fear. From the time I was little, my parents shared who God was with me and the power of using God in my life. I grew up going to a Catholic school from kindergarten through high school. My parents always talked about their faith and the importance of having a relationship with God. They reminded me to not fear but rather *use* the gifts God has given me to help those around me and shine light on who God is in my life. In college, I remember seeing girls who were literally nuts for Jesus. They would listen to praise and worship music, they would go to Bible studies, and these were the nicest women in the sorority. It clicked for me one day: these girls are the way they are because they're fully connected to Jesus. I watched from afar then started to listen to the music, picked up my Bible, later met my husband, who was seeking Jesus in a real and powerful way, and since then my life has never been the same. Maintaining a relationship with God empowered me. As hard as I worked in school, my new business seemed effortless and fun.

It was at this point I realized I didn't need the approval of an educational institution to know where I excelled. At 19 years old, I gifted myself with being okay with Cs and maximized my potential as a new business owner. God groomed me for this position long ago; I reminded myself often of my stuffed monkeys that lined my bed to learn a shuffle step or the neighborhood children joining me in the summer dancing in my front yard. I finally gave myself permission to do what God called me to do, and there I found my joy, immense joy. I remember walking into the daycare the first day of Tippi Toes class with a stack of flyers, the boom box from my dorm room, and electrical tape I'd use for dance lines. Once I turned on some music from when I was growing up -- think "Splish Splash" by Bobby Darin and "Little Ol' Cowgirl" by the Dixie Chicks -- it didn't take long for the kids to start following along, dancing, and having fun. And I remember Karissa, the daycare's director, smiling and nodding her approval. I knew I was onto something. I was thrilled to return to these kids week after week, and I was even more excited to pocket some checks made out to Tippi Toes. A single spark, one idea or one thought, can change the trajectory of our lives when we put action behind it. When we are faithful and obedient to His plans, greatness always follows. That day, I didn't realize this spark would define my entire future, but through hard work, obedience, and passion, God turned Tippi Toes into something so much greater than anything I could ever conjure myself. Now talking about my early days with my business, it is evident to me that in every piece, big and small, God was there, faithfully guiding me in this journey.

Take action

Create space for focus

It's so important to be in tune with yourself and know what you, as the unique individual you are, need in order to get work done. When I work, my environment has to have the perfect conditions for me to feel like I can accomplish the task at hand. I sit in total silence at my home desk when my family is gone, sunshine streaming through the window, an organized desktop, my phone set to Do Not Disturb, and the day's tasks outlined in my day planner. I still have to fight my attention deficit disorder (ADD), which has gotten much better over the years. If the room isn't completely quiet, I easily drift into any distraction that is in front of me and have to intentionally pull myself back to focus. I can be seen getting up from my desk in the middle of typing a word, going to empty the dishwasher, talking on the phone, making doodles all over the paper, and even staring out the window daydreaming of what my current project could do for our company -- making myself snap back to it. I have come a long way learning that I work best in the morning until about 3 p.m., and that for the first fifteen minutes of any project, I am like a wiggly toddler stuck in a car seat until I get in my groove. I give myself grace most days but also don't allow myself to leave my desk until I finish what I sat down to complete. I used to overschedule myself and would put much more on my schedule than could be done well. Over time, I've learned that after the initial fifteen minutes of getting adjusted, I get into a deep rhythm and my project really starts taking stride.

Your work environment needs might look wholly different from mine, but the one thing I know for sure we have in common is that none of us accomplishes anything without focus. To play a major role in making your future one of continued promise and triumphs, it's absolutely essential to create the time and space to get down to business. What is something you want to try but haven't fully engaged in yet? What is getting in the way of you being focused on this goal? How can you set aside 30 minutes a day to focus solely on this dream? What are your patterns? Best time of day to work and best ways to focus?

Here are some ideas:

- get up one hour earlier

- write out your day in advance so you run your day and it doesn't run you

- remove an inconsequential to-do in your day and replace it with your goal

Get an accountability partner who will encourage you daily and possibly join you on the journey to maximize your focus. The truth is none of us 100% knows our ideas will work out, so why not try it anyway? My idea of paying for my car payment by waitressing was the best idea I had at the time. It worked for a while, until of course it didn't. Getting fired was one of the best things to ever happen to me in my life. That "failure," as some people might call getting fired, catapulted me into a life I never could have planned on paper, that nudge allowing me to try something I might never would have. God took my moment of defeat and turned it into something amazing. Try, try really hard at what you are doing. If we try hard and it doesn't work out, that moment just groomed us for something greater.

CHAPTER 2

I Have a Business. Now What?

How to succeed in business by trying, trying, trying.

What happened next in my business was truly amazing and really fun. Like a family tree that starts with the trunk and grows limb by limb, all thriving by the same root, so did my business. KinderCare, the trunk, had nine branches in the Oklahoma City area. Operating from both excitement and some trepidation, I talked to the assistant director, Kim, about what it would look like to take Tippi Toes to her other locations. She smiled and said, "Sarah, you need to do it!" The confidence in her voice gave me the courage to ask for the point of contact at each location. She topped that request by saying she would personally call each location to recommend Tippi Toes. I can't stress enough how valuable it is to have people like this rooting for your success early on.

The way Tippi Toes worked was I would walk into each daycare with my boom box, electrical tape for dancing lines, and a smile. I wore my black spaghetti strap leotard, black wraparound ballet skirt, pink cutoff ballet tights, and ballet slippers: not your typical sorority girl outfit. I'd greet the school's teachers and directors, then walk to the empty classroom they had assigned to me that day. Typically, I'd need to move tables, stack chairs, sweep up stray Cheerios from snack time, and hide as many toys as possible so the kids remained focused on class. Then I walked from classroom to classroom with my teacher notebook -- the ones I remember opening up on Christmas morning when I asked Santa for teacher supplies -- to gather the three- and four-year-old children whose parents had enrolled in my class. On our Tippi Toes, we would "Tippi Toe" our little feet into my empty classroom, where our world of imagination would come alive. Ballet, tap, and jazz were all woven throughout our magical adventure. My goal each class was to bring the children the best 45 minutes of their day. We danced, sang songs, pretended we were in magical forests or even in a different country. I would crawl on the floor, prance around like a deer, jump like a bunny, slither on that sticky daycare floor pretending to be a snake. You name it, and if a smile would be the return investment, I was all in. I remember the joy I got from Miss Shelly's dance classes when I was little and how she complimented each student by name every single week. I loved this feeling of recognition, and so I included it in my dance classes, too. After an energetic 45-minute dance class, we would Tippi Toe back to each classroom for the students to rejoin their classes. I'd put my room back together, thank the director, and be on my way.

My classes grew from five students per school to twelve in just one month, like new leaves sprouting during the spring. Each student paid $20 a month. As I expanded to other locations, I quickly learned how to drive sales myself with the dreaded cold call. Who *doesn't* hate cold calling? Well, I'm no different. But I switched my thought process to begin simply offering up an opportunity I genuinely didn't want families to miss. If they signed up with Tippi Toes, their kids could start their school day with music and movement! By incorporating dance into the day, parents could remove the hassle of shuttling their kids to dance class after a long day.

By the end of my first operating year, and while still a college sophomore, I secured all nine KinderCare locations in Oklahoma City. Each class held steady with an average of twelve kids. I worked nine hours a week and reached more than one hundred students. *That* is how you maximize your time! Now I could afford my car payment plus gas money, which I thought was pretty cool. Then it became a wildfire of fun: I called Norman Public Schools and set up a meeting to talk to the afterschool programs director. The district had nineteen elementary schools at the time and asked if I could host dance classes for the students after the school day. *No problem* was my first reaction, not wanting to bypass this opportunity. Little did they know, I hadn't hired any help yet, so this would be a true business test. As a college student, I pretty much felt like I was rich. And I couldn't believe I had all of these kids trusting in and dancing with me. My passion took over, and I constantly thought of different ways to build upon my venture's success, like by holding periodic recitals. Being a new, inexperienced businesswoman meant I needed to get my business straight. For the first three years of its existence, I viewed Tippi Toes like, well ... a babysitting job. So I never set it up as an official business. Eek!

Please learn from my mistake that this is a bad idea. I attribute this oversight to my innocence -- remember, I was still only 19! -- and me not recognizing that I did, in fact, have a business. One big sign should have been when I set up a bank account so parents could write checks for my classes. For the first year, the checks went straight to me: Sarah Lowery, rather than my business name. Receiving my first piece of mail at my sorority house addressed to Sarah Lowery DBA Tippi Toes made me positively giddy.

I quickly learned the government doesn't care if you didn't mean to start a business; the fact is it *was* started, and I owed $1,700 in the form of taxes. I called the richest young person I knew, someone making an obscene amount of money right out of college, and asked him what I should do. I mean, that makes sense, right? Another rookie move. His advice? Pay the bills, keep $10,000 in my bank account to save for taxes, and spend the rest. I listened. I paid the outstanding taxes and spent the next year saving money to hit the $10,000 mark. Once I reached that magic number, I bought anything and everything I wanted or felt like I needed. Anthropologie became my favorite store, and I wouldn't flinch at dropping $500 on a trip inside. I didn't hire an accountant. I didn't make a budget. I feared the government because I didn't understand the system. I just felt like the powers that be would take more than I planned for, so oddly enough, I just didn't plan. I blindly moved ahead pretending it wasn't going to happen. It was dumb, and I wish I would have stopped, learned, and understood, but at that time, I just didn't. Another rookie move. There were no financial systems in place, and money wasn't being accounted for. I figured it was working, since I was making a profit, and I didn't think to ask anyone else for advice. Oh, if I could only go back and sit myself down at 19 to tell me all the things I wish I would have known! I would say something like this: "Sarah, officially set up your business! Get an accountant who will explain things so you understand how to run your enterprise. Know the formula and schedule for paying taxes, but don't fear the process. Part of having pride in the business you started means not pretending like it isn't a real business. Own the parts of your business you don't know, and seek wise counsel. Sarah, just because someone is rich, it doesn't mean they are wise. Go with the wise ones; they will steer you right for the long term."

The beauty in this story is that I did end up learning it all, but it took some hard lessons, late payments, seeing my bank account in the red, and some tears -- or maybe lots of tears. Maybe an ocean of tears is right where you are today. Zechariah 4:10 reads, "Do not despise these small beginnings, for the Lord rejoices to see the work begin, to see the plumb line in Zerubbabel's hand." Truth be told, I despised this part of my beginning for a long time. I felt like I really failed as a business owner. I felt like I didn't have a firm grasp on what I was doing when it came to accounting, and so I believed myself to be a loser. I wanted to be in class, teach dance to the kids, but I didn't want to face the "hard" part of my business. But starting a business is hard, knowing what to do next is hard, feeling alone is hard. Before it becomes unmanageable, ask for help! When I finally did, accepting the accounting side was the fuel to run my business and deserved a professional controlling it, Tippi Toes moved forward faster.

Take action

Embrace urgency

Had I known Tippi Toes would become a worldwide franchise, maybe I would have finessed the perfect plan entailing business classes, a professional website, handout materials, and a better pitch right from the start! The urgency in my spirit forced me to overlook details, yet this impulse has been my business plan ever since. You don't need to wait on the ideal situation to create movement toward your goals. Just *go*. (Yes, it can be scary. And uncomfortable. Please refer to the image in Chapter 1, and remind yourself to Face The Fear.) I didn't realize this would be such a huge moment in my life. I simply took action, and it came from a place of urgency, that urgency I can only describe as a gift from God.

What lights you up inside? What do people tell you you're good at? Start there. Throw one thousand ideas against the wall, and then *get moving*.

- What is holding you back from moving forward?

- Where do you need a little more urgency in your life and a little less planning?

- Who is someone wise you've seen run a successful business from whom you can glean wisdom?

CHAPTER 3

Partnering with Others (and God)

Entrepreneurs make it up as they go.

In a major coup, I landed the Norman Public Schools deal. Eleven of their schools would experience Tippi Toes starting the next semester, with the remaining schools to be added the semester after that. With a full college class schedule and these new dance classes -- resulting in a total of 20 daycares and schools -- I knew it was time to hire someone for my teaching staff. If you'll remember, I was still just 19, a sophomore in college who had been fired the year before. Apart from my OTB waitressing job, I had never been on a job interview myself, yet I was getting ready to interview people for a potential teaching role with me at Tippi Toes. I didn't have a business background, understand how interviews should take place, or even know the right questions to ask. Being young has extreme advantages, because guess what? I didn't care. I honestly didn't even think about trying to look or sound professional because I didn't have time to worry about it: I had a growing business and needed help fast. I put up an ad in the college dorm rooms and got only one phone call.

"Hello, I am calling about the dance teacher job you have available," said the sweet voice on the other end of the line.

I covered the receiver and yelled out to Chanda, my roommate at the time. "This is someone who wants to work for Tippi Toes!"

Chanda screamed, and I screamed, then I got back on the phone with my most adult voice and decided right then to become a professional interviewer. I asked:

1. What is your full name?

2. Have you ever danced before?

3. Do you like kids?

4. What is your favorite color?

5. What hours do you have available?

Aren't you impressed with those interview questions? Her answers went like this: My name is Casey; yes, I have danced; yes, I do like kids; I love the color pink; and I can work anytime in the afternoon. *Thank God!* I thought. *She loves pink, too!* Little did she know I had one more test for her before she was hired.

After I hung up the phone, Chanda and I danced around our rental house, full of excitement that I would potentially have someone helping me with Tippi Toes. We celebrated like we'd won an enormous prize and kept high-fiving. Then Chanda asked what we should ask Casey during our face-to-face interview. In my truest fashion, I continued toasting to the moment and decided to prepare questions later.

Well, later came, and Casey was on her way to our house. What a professional place to host an interview right? Again, this is where my naiveté came in handy. I had prepared a multiple-choice test for her to take as part of her interview along with oral questions to be answered. Chanda, my boyfriend Adam, and I comprised the hiring committee. The three of us sat in a row on the couch across from a chair we'd placed in the center of the room for her. What were we thinking with this interrogation scene? We planned to fire questions at her one after the other to make the process seem "formal." I don't remember our questions, but if she answered them anything like in her phone interview, I am sure she passed with flying colors. You guys, how crazy is that? I am trying to hire her to teach, five hours a week at minimum wage, and am making her take a thirty-question multiple choice test at my house and interview with three people. The craziest part of this story is I had zero other applicants. *Zero.* By the grace of God, she took the job. Casey, also a University of Oklahoma student, worked for Tippi Toes throughout college and led me to numerous other great teachers by sharing her love of Tippi Toes and dancing with her friends and sorority sisters.

The following semester, classes continued to boom, adding the remaining eight district schools in addition to five new locations. I held interviews again, and this time, I stepped it up. I rented out a room at the Norman Community Center, placing a table in the center of the room with eight chairs surrounding it. I begged my family to help with the interview process, and they agreed, knowing what this growing business meant to me. My mom, dad, and Megan drove two hours from Tulsa, and my older sister Jennie joined from 30 minutes away in Oklahoma City. Just like the first time, Chanda and Adam would be there, too. We changed our interrogators from three of us to now seven. From the advertisements I had posted around campus, we had five girls wanting a position, and, you guessed it, five was the number of teachers I needed. At the end of a long night full of questions, confirmation that they knew dance positions, reviewing their background dance experience, a few tests, and many conversations, they were hired: Kari, Merry, Ashley, Brittany, and Suzie. This group, along with Casey, remains my favorite hires because they just believed in me and in Tippi Toes at the earliest stage, connected with what we were trying to do, and were fully on board. They allowed me to train them while I was still learning myself. We'd meet in the new wing of my sorority house, and they'd dance alongside me, making sure they had the dances down for class.

Choreography is my jam! It comes naturally to me. When the music starts up, I can put together a dance in a matter of minutes. I filled spiral notebooks with dance after dance. The teachers I hired would read my handwritten notes, watch me dance a few times, and then join me to go over the steps. We'd run to the Theta house copy machine to make copies of my notes so they could practice on their own time, too. Since many times the girls were also teaching with me throughout the week as part of their training, they'd get to know the material well. Most of our classes had anywhere from 12-15 students dancing. This meant two teachers for each class: one as the lead teacher and the other as the assistant. The lead would be responsible for making sure the class ran smoothly and the dancers learned their material. While the assistant was the shoe-tier, the tear-wiper, the bathroom-runner, and anything else that needed to be addressed. The time I spent outside of actual class with my teachers was about five extra hours a week. I loved this time with them because I learned their hearts, and that is where our friendships formed. Since that time, we have hired hundreds of amazing teachers throughout our company. Luckily for them, the hiring process has changed considerably, and the choreography notes are much simpler to read, but the heartbeat of the company remains the same.

There wasn't a roadmap for me when I started Tippi Toes. Entrepreneurs make it up as they go. We have to; we don't have a choice. We guess based on what we think will work best and learn from what goes wrong. I knew at this point in my business I needed help to maximize my efforts and continue to turn a profit. The five girls I hired allowed Tippi Toes to grow faster, as they took on several classes teaching different hours than Casey and me throughout the week. Having a total of seven of us dancing around the greater Oklahoma City area, each teaching a minimum of ten kids per class, was a clear way to continue to grow this business. With each dancer paying $20 a month for one class per week, the numbers added up fast. I paid each instructor $8 for each class they taught. At the time, it was much higher than the state's minimum wage, which was $5.15. They were happy, and we were all making money. I knew the right action done with the right team over a period of time would equal success. Hiring help wasn't only an option; it was a *must* in order to see growth.

I learned I must have faith in my efforts and value to get other people on board, too. The fact that I wasn't good in school couldn't be the excuse holding me back.

Being a C student for a long time allowed me to convince myself I wouldn't be successful. I literally felt stupid in school. From my early years in Sister Eileen's third-grade classroom, I would get up to blow my nose when she started asking math questions, just to avoid being called on. I was ashamed that school came hard for me. This embarrassment was something I instilled in my own mind, since my parents constantly reminded me and my sisters of our worth. But the mind is powerful. I would hide my report card and get busted when my sisters turned in their As and Bs. I'd sheepishly hand over my own report card with tears in my eyes. I have learned good grades don't guarantee adult success. In fact, I think my difficulty in school allowed me to work from a different gear. To keep up with my grades, I had to study longer, get a tutor, stay late after school to ask more questions, and even attend summer school. This turned into a benefit for my business because it gave me a familiarity with pushing on even when things don't seem to come naturally. God won't let us use our weaknesses as an excuse for not doing what He is asking. We have to just go, knowing that God has gone before us.

The confidence I had in Tippi Toes early on motivated Casey to join me. My class numbers were evidence Tippi Toes worked, giving me the nerve to expand. It doesn't take a lot to keep you going when you want to succeed with every fiber of your being. Although I did get into many Kinder Cares right off the bat, I got rejected, too. As a teenager making cold calls, walking into a preschool with a vague business plan bolstered by a dream, I was often laughed at. I remember driving up to Broadview Education Center, which sat just off campus, an easy walk from class. I walked in with a bright smile, knowing exactly the day this location would fit into my schedule.

The lady who somewhat greeted me immediately asked, "What are you sellin'?" in a twangy Oklahoma accent.

I replied, "Nothing, ma'am. I want to give your students an opportunity to dance while at school."

She looked me square in the eye and said, "I don't know why we would be interested in something like that."

Feeling defeated but also persistent, I continued. "It is an opportunity for families to not have to race around in the evening to dance class but rather get quality family time together." I didn't want her to "win" by making me feel bad. That's right, I am competitive, too. I just needed to get past her to see the center's director, and I knew I could convince them they needed Tippi Toes.

Then the woman said something that defeated me, the exact reason I relate to people when they say they don't like cold calls. Her words: "Your idea won't work here. Families won't like it. We are simply not interested."

I politely smiled and walked back outside but had trouble leaving the loss behind me. I lost because I failed to show her what we could do for the families. I let it bother me longer than it should have. This is why running a business, starting something new and being bold, is hard: without knowing you, without understanding you, people will shape opinions about you in an instant, and their judgment can etch a scar on your heart. It did mine, so after I got over that damage, I vowed to never ever let anyone tell me why Tippi Toes wouldn't work. Instead, I used that energy to find the schools and locations that would open their arms to us, allow us to share our gifts and impact their students and families in a positive and beautiful way. I turned the wound she gave me that day into fuel, refining my pitch, better handling rejection, and moving on. I turned my negative thoughts into positive thoughts that would push my business forward.

REFOCUS YOUR FEAR

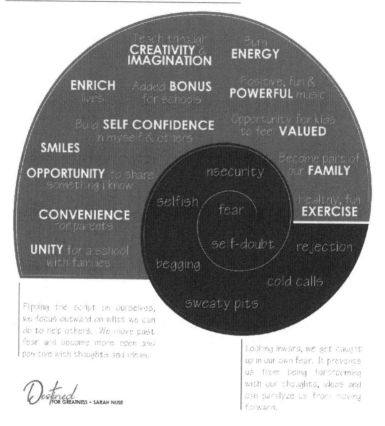

Flipping the script on ourselves, we focus outward on what we can do to help others. We move past fear and become more open and positive with thoughts and ideas.

Destined FOR GREATNESS - SARAH NUSE

Looking inward, we get caught up in our own fear. It prevents us from being forthcoming with our thoughts, ideas and can paralyze us from moving forward.

When you encounter doubt or judgment from others, might I recommend you flip the script? Allow yourself to see the value in what you're doing instead of the negative thoughts swirling deep inside. Take a look at the Refocus Your Fear Graphic. The dark colors show what my inner self was fighting with: insecurity, fear, self-doubt, and so much more just absolute junk. When I got out of my own way and started to think of how Tippi Toes could impact others, the world became light. In the end, the rejection that hounded me made me trust in my mission and Tippi Toes's potential even more strongly. When we believe in what we are doing and remind ourselves daily it isn't about our path but rather our effect on others, we can push our dreams so much farther.

You can do the same. Not everyone will like your business, either. People will judge your product, tell you another way you can do it, or say they have seen it done better elsewhere. Take it all with a grain of salt, friend. You have worked hard for what you've created, and the world needs your voice, your ideas, and your drive. I *knew* Tippi Toes was working. I saw it, and I experienced it. That faith I had from seeing Tippi Toes work was just enough to keep me hungry for more.

Rejection can suppress the hunger for development. Stunted, we won't advance. Distraction is an indulgence in which we can't afford to wallow. Our time here is precious, and if God created us to be powerful and strong, then He did not create us to wallow in self-pity.

He designed us with a resilient spirit, if only we could access it. Yet you *can* access it by taking action. Let's say you need investors for your food truck plans. Resolve to make one phone call this week, and do it first thing Monday morning; don't delay. You need a book agent? Resolve to send out your proposal every day until it happens. That's right, *every day*. You want to be a top seller in your company? Do 10% more every day than the top person is doing in your company. Remember that daily actions, even just one, every single day will take you a step closer to success.

And pray! God wants to partner with each of us. Often, we get busy working out our own plans and schedule that we forget to include Him. I have been guilty of this more times than I would like to admit. Partnering with God also helps us ignore the devil's doubt. At this point with Tippi Toes, I forgot to trust in Him, knowing He had gone before me and laid a path that would bring my life and my family so much purpose. The second I heard someone say no to what I offered their school, I began to second-guess it all, everything I had worked for. I didn't run to God with it; instead, I wrestled, I cried, and I worried. My worry sounded like, "What if what that lady said was true, and what if people start dropping from my classes, and what if teachers don't continue to enjoy Tippi Toes?" The "what if" list of brand-new concerns continued on. When we turn over our worries, doubts, and what ifs to God, He calms our hearts in the middle of our own little storm by giving us peace.

I was reminded God does this a few weeks after my first sting of rejection. Dear Chanda, she knew how badly it bothered me. So she matter-of-factly said, "Okay, Sarah, sit down." We sat on our twin-size beds eating SweeTARTS until we were sick, both with our "blankies" in hand (pretty sure we were the only two college girls still with blankies), and talked about the worry that was over taking me. "So what if all the terrible things you are making up happen? Play them out with me," she prompted. She was wise beyond her years, that Chanda, especially at 19. She spoke words of love and truth over my life and my little business. She reminded me that I was in line with God's path, and although neither of us knew at the time that Tippi Toes would be my forever job, she spoke as if it were all meant to be. When my friend shined God's light back on my business, which I had allowed doubt to dim, the confidence bubbled back up inside of me.

Tippi Toes was growing, and my sister Megan graduated high school in Tulsa and joined me to become an Oklahoma Sooner. She volunteered to enter students' names in an Excel document to keep track of attendance, contact information, and payments. She did this at first to help get me organized, as she was much more organized by nature than me, though nothing compared to our older sister Jennie. While Megan's world would be tidy, Jennie's was spotless and mine ... well, let's just call it well-lived-in. Megan could tell I struggled under the piles of enrollment papers on my desk. Just as Jennie would come and help me clean my room when I was little after I tore it apart looking for my ballet slippers, now Megan swooped in to help straighten my business. Thank goodness God gave me sisters -- regimented sisters, at that. As Megan lifted the burden on my desk, her job grew into more tasks that would help the company progress.

After finishing her freshman year at the University of Oklahoma, Megan switched schools to follow her career path of becoming a dietician. While at Oklahoma State, just an hour from me in Stillwater, she started to teach Tippi Toes classes during what downtime she had. Having also grown up dancing, she was a natural. Over the phone, we talked about new daycare centers, schools to approach, and how our students were doing, and our Stillwater expansion excited us. Determined to make money and make an impact, Megan grew my dance program during her college years. Studying to become a dietician was a lot different than my college experience when I just asked what it would take to get me out. Megan was driven in school and always excelled. She pushed herself to understand what she was learning to the very core and expected A's from herself, needing to maintain a certain GPA to get her master's. I knew her future was bright but assumed having her master's would take her far from Tippi Toes.

I stayed in Norman when I graduated in 2002 to solidify Tippi Toes ... okay, because my boyfriend Adam was a year younger and still in school; maybe that was my real reason. His master's program took him to Wichita State the following year, and I went to Kansas City to live with my grandmother, Gram, conveniently only three hours from Adam. In Kansas City, I spread my wings and expanded Tippi Toes, bringing on 16 new locations that first year while still operating the Oklahoma City and Stillwater areas from a distance. I hired Kristin, a young bubbly girl who danced for the Avila University dance team in Kansas City, to assist me in my classes. She was the perfect addition to our Tippi Toes team. As I got comfortable with this new arrangement of managing my dream team of six dance teachers from afar, I knew I could take an even bigger step. It was a cold December night in Wichita, Kansas, and Adam and I were at his apartment watching the 2003 Heisman trophy announcement when he asked me to be his wife, and I said yes.

After our wedding, we moved to Corpus Christi, Texas, where Adam would start his baseball career with the Corpus Christi Hooks. Kristin, my amazing teacher in Kansas City, was eager to be fully in charge of the operation and took it over with excitement, teaching all 16 classes and adding four more to make it an even 20. Tippi Toes was on the move again, and I planned to expand it in our new city. The truth of it was I got scared again. I was a newlywed, I now had new responsibilities as a wife. Adam and I had never lived together before, so figuring out the details of what this would look like took some adjusting, and I put stress on myself. A clean house, a home cooked meal on the table when he walked in from work: oh yes, I tried to be June Cleaver from *Leave It to Beaver*, minus the kids.

All the while, I was managing Oklahoma and Kansas City. I froze in fear of biting off another task. The truth of it, which I can see now, is that I was good at what I was doing. I let fear creep in and tell me I would fail in front of my new husband. If I did fail, I wouldn't be contributing to our family. It would be so visible to him and in our bank account. None of it was true, but somehow I sat in it and believed it, and it froze me. It's silly because Adam had been there the entire way navigating Tippi Toes with me, but I think we all go through this at points in our life. Things are smooth sailing, and then we let our mind play tricks on us and not allow ourselves to live fully in what God called us to do. There was a preschool one block from our new home, and it took me six months to walk in and share Tippi Toes. Still carrying the rejection from my cold call so long ago made me not want to take a step forward. I focused more on the nonacceptance than all the success I had before. Why do we do that? The funny thing is this school would earn us thirty-six Tippi Toes dancers once I finally had the courage to just walk inside and ask.

Looking back, I see this is where character is developed, along with wisdom and discernment. Virtues are given to us after the messy. After the tears. And after the heartache. I celebrate knowing that the Lord directs our steps. If we embrace the toughest moments, we can trust God will direct us to His ways. Sometimes I roll my eyes. Sometimes I look up with a snarl on my face. But then I know to reach for resilience because I know it's there, because I have used it before. I'm reminded His ways are always so much greater and higher than what we could ever imagine. Proverbs 20:24 reads, "The Lord directs our steps, so why try to understand everything along the way?" When I reflect on many of my business moments, I see I'm just running hard, so hard that I don't have time to analyze whether an idea even works. I think part of that is not having a solid plan in place. I have found when I do have a plan and my steps are mapped out, my nose gets out of joint if I don't see what I think should be happening on paper happening in real life. I sit, study, reflect, review, and forget that *just moving forward* is a good game plan. (Have you heard that saying "Done is better than perfect"?)

So why *do* we try to understand everything along the way? It's human nature, I guess. Those moments when we crumble, get fired, or suffer a stinging loss open us to an opportunity to grow closer to God, view our situation in a new light, and make the most of what we were handed. For me, I love reflecting back on situations, people, and experiences and seeing God so clearly within them. Getting fired was a gift to me; God clearly was positioning me for something so much better. My bank account in the red at the time made me feel like I was suffocating, but today seeing it in the black makes me thankful for the growth in business knowledge. The "no" from a location I so badly wanted was God's protection over me to teach me and grow me to be a tough and fiery sales girl. I choose to view every slump, failure, detour as an opportunity to see where God wants to direct my steps. If we fail to see God in these moments, these moments are failed. When we look back, the details of God become so clear. Look to

God, because there is such greatness when we are held in His arms and guided by His gentle hand. God has such special plans for you and me. We have got to rest in the understanding that God had a hold on our future long before we could possibly dream of what we want.

Before I knew what I wanted my life to be like, when I thought I just needed to scrounge up enough money to make a car payment, God had already written all the excitement that was going to happen now and is still yet to come. Do you want to think of something really fun? God knows how your story ends up: every detail, every twist, and every turn. He knows every single victory, every single heartache, every single person you will meet and all that comes between. That desire you have in your heart, He put it there and will complete it for you. He promises us that all we must do is go. Scripture says so: "And I am certain that God, who began a good work within you, will continue his work until it is finally finished on the day when Christ Jesus returns," reads Philippians 1:6.

I had no idea what getting fired from OTB would do to my life, and yet it was the best gift I could have received. What do you feel like you have learned in hindsight of a situation that didn't seem to go your way? Have you had your life take a sharp, uncomfortable turn only to find out there was great purpose? You may be sitting in that position now. We are always becoming someone, growing, changing, learning. Each step -- or misstep, for that matter -- allows us to become the best or worst version of ourselves. It's our attitude, our outlook, and our choices that determine how we land. Let me encourage you to hold on. Your life, it has a purpose. You are destined for greatness. God designed you to be unique and completely authentic, and He is the God of extreme creativity and wants to pour blessing on your life. That sharp turn you're navigating is part of your story. Later, when you share it, people will find you because of how you finished, but they will relate to you because of what is right here, in the tough stuff. Hang in there -- God is writing an incredible story with your life.

Take action

Celebrate the steps, even the hard ones

Had everything gone as planned, nothing would have gone right. I would not be the person I am today, and neither would you. I would have not gotten fired because I would never have planned for that. Had I not been fired then, I wouldn't be entrusted with the business I have now. None of us wants to go through hard moments; let's be honest, it totally stinks. No, I don't like being financially strapped at 19, but guess what that taught me? To be wise with my money and the way I handle it. It took me seeing my bank account in the negative to know I never wanted it to go there again. We have the gift of growing wise when we learn from our mistakes and adjust where we need to. So consider it a gift when you get those unplanned sharp hard turns that are sometimes unbearable. Lean into those moments and know that growth and wisdom often follow.

CHAPTER 4

Better Together

The trick to belaying is being tied to a solid rock. In our

lives, the rock is the stuff that matters most.

From cheering at basketball games, to towing the boat to the lake for the weekend, I was blessed with a family that did everything together. We were taught at a young age that our best friends were built in: each other. Often, my two sisters and I put on dance shows in our living room. My mom would DJ, spinning much-requested Michael Jackson songs, and my dad would hold his arm up high with a flashlight, putting the spotlight on each of us in turn. Night after night, song after song, my parents would hoop and holler and encourage us to shine.

In addition to being my built-in best friends, my sisters are also my colleagues. My older sister Jennie and I are only 18 months apart, so we've grown into adult life sharing so many of the big-ticket experiences: getting married around the same time, setting up homes, and motherhood. Jennie is loyal and fierce. She takes the role of big sister seriously. When I was homesick in college, she'd show up to my dorm with a Classic 50's green apple slush with gummy bears, knowing just how to bring a smile to my face. My inbox is known to contain forwards from her on how to raise a tween, having a kid who isn't addicted to technology, and so on. Jennie is the buttoned-up sister who has her oil changed on time and her children's physicals completed before sports season starts, and when it comes to her leaving town, she is the girl with the list of notes to make it easy on the rest of us. She thrives on family time and has a unique special relationship with each of my kids. Instead of giving me gifts, she gifts me with her time to help me organize a spot in my house, and she does it meticulously. She loves a good laugh, traditions, and making others feel special -- namely me. She is also a Tippi Toes franchise owner.

Megan, the youngest of the three of us, is the family comedian who got away with more than Jennie and I combined. Three years younger than me, she was the all-star athlete and academic brains in our family. She is fiercely protective and thrived during family game night. From the time I started teaching kids dance lessons in my front yard, Megan was by my side helping. Her job started with taking the dancers to the bathroom. Glamorous, I know. But when you're nine and your sister is twelve, that is just the kind of job you get. Years later, she went from working for Tippi Toes part-time (remember those Excel documents she totally rocked?) to finishing her master's in dietetics and completing her last hospital internship, before having the revelation that Tippi Toes was her future. She was engaged, and she and Chris were getting married and moving to Cincinnati. She saw me working full-time with Tippi Toes and managing three states' worth of dance classes, and she knew she could do it, too. Megan turned in her lab coat for a tutu and poured her heart and soul into Tippi Toes from that day forward.

Although we'd worked together on a part-time basis during college, it was like I hit the jackpot when Megan came on full-time with Tippi Toes. All her hours of studying, stressing over tests, and working in the

SARAH NUSE

hospital came down to her following her passion: Tippi Toes. I was honored to have her faith in me. Sisters -- in business! My business partner and my counterpart dream chaser. I could list all the adorable things about Megan, but for the sake of this business book, let me get to her astounding capacity to spin plates, juggle balls, answer questions, and organize it all while sipping a fountain Diet Coke and telling jokes to make me smile. That's my girl Megan. From our early days in our front yard, we worked well together. We rarely ruffle each other's feathers and have been known to say the exact same thing at the exact same time in response to someone's question. It's an insane display of synchronization. When you have someone who is like-minded, is passionate, and shares the same vision, what a bountiful harvest you reap.

A goal or dream isn't nearly as rewarding and you don't get nearly as far as quickly when going it alone. What I have learned is it is much better to do it alongside those you love, but my advice is one that many people disagree with. If you Google "Should I go into business with family?" you will get a list several pages long of people against bringing family into business. In fact,

Entrepreneur magazine has one article bluntly titled "25 Reasons Why Hiring Your Relatives Is an Even Worse Idea Than You Suspected." [1] The article, however, pinpoints key reasons for this success and failure, and there's one that Megan and I have stuck to since day one: play to each other's strengths. The *Entrepreneur* article, written in 2017, compares the Disney brothers (Walt and Roy) to the Kellogg brothers (Will and John). The Disneys played to their strengths to help build a great company The Kellogg brothers were unable to set aside ego, unable to communicate, and not willing to allow the other partner to give input for success.

God knew I needed Megan and she needed me, long before Tippi Toes was a thought in our minds. We still help each other grow, cheer each other on, and push one another to never stop doing what God has called us to do. Megan's go-to text to me: "You got this, Bear." I, on the other hand, am the one to pick up the phone and preach to her about what she's capable of. We are each other's source for pep talks calling out the

---

[1] John Rampton, "25 Reasons Why Hiring Your Relatives Is an Even Worse Idea Than You Suspected," *Entrepreneur*, July 7, 2017, https://www.entrepreneur.com/article/296592

greatness we see in the other. We are sisters first and business partners second.

We once had a big meeting with a franchise company, and that morning, my 8-month-old daughter Lucy got sick. I couldn't miss the meeting, but I'd be danged to not be with my sick baby. I was torn, not sure what to do. I called Megan, and she simply said "Bring her, Bear. We will divide and conquer." And that's exactly what we did. Lucy would need her medicine, so I'd pop out of my chair, feed her, comfort her, and walk back into the meeting. The next hour, Lucy would get fussy, and without hesitation, Megan would give me the look to go ahead and finish what I was doing. Family first.

This day is etched in my mind because not only did Megan help me combine my family and work commitments, but she also made it seem like she was happy to make it work and got the better end of the deal. "Bear, I got to rock Lucy while you had to sit and listen to the attorney. Winning!" she said with a smile on her face. As years have gone on and more additions to our family have been made, Megan and I can bob and weave each other's family and business needs all while landing on the same page. It is common for Megan and me to have a Zoom meeting with a franchise owner, hang up at its conclusion, then call each other again for me to see my niece Harper's latest painting or Stella and Kate's latest dance move. It comes with the territory and reminds us when we are grinding away that family is our top priority.

When I talk about partners in business, I can't forget to include my partner in life. One evening in 2010, my husband Adam and I were zoning out in front of *Shark Tank* once our daughters Lucy and Lola were finally asleep at the same time. We high-fived each other because this particular night's bedtime went smoothly. (Don't you love that rare occasion? It's a grown-up's birthday wish come true.) Adam, with a glass of wine in hand, and I curled up on the couch, me with my feet on his lap. Our golden night of relaxation had begun, and to celebrate, we started watching a new-to-us show. As I stared at the TV, I pointed out all the amazing things happening on the show. The one that caught me was Grease Monkey Wipes, a simple product that would wipe away grease from *anything*. The "sharks" salivated over this product. They all wanted in. What was it about this simple product that excited them so much? I thought about Tippi Toes and our profit margin and wondered if maybe, just maybe, they would react the same way. Adam appeared to vaguely be watching next to me, flicking his eyes back and forth between the TV and his computer screen.

"Adam, look," I said, pointing at Grease Monkey Wipes. "Adam, listen to that."

No response from my husband. Then, a few months later, I got a call.

"Hello Sarah, this is Roberta from ABC's *Shark Tank.* We would like to talk to you about being on our show."

JAW. DROP. Excuse me, *what?* Immediately, I called Adam. "Adam, *Shark Tank* found us. You know, that show we were watching."

"Oh, good," he replied, unfazed. "They got my submission for Tippi Toes."

Adam never told me that the night I thought he wasn't paying attention to the show, he was, in fact, on his computer signing up Tippi Toes to appear on a reality show celebrating entrepreneurs like his wife.

Adam is always the first to cheer me on or offer up a crazy idea he believes I can knock out of the park. When Tippi Toes was a baby, he asked what my goal was. I smiled at him and said, "To keep paying for that car." (Don't think I didn't remain head over heels for that Toyota Celica the whole time it was in my life! My pride couldn't be contained.)

"How many students does that monthly car payment take?" he asked. He grabbed a piece of paper from my printer, pulled a chair up next to my desk, and began doodling. It was a simple graph to help me see and keep track of my growth. He taped this doodle to my bathroom mirror so I would see it every day. He handed me a pink magic marker. "Color a block each day as a new student enrolls."

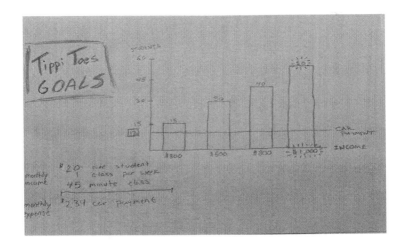

He literally has said to me, "Sarah, there is nothing you can't do." What a peach, right? To have this kind of support from my husband allows me to believe I can move mountains. So with his help, I try.

I called Megan to share the news about *Shark Tank*. She screamed, I screamed. The show required a video submission and, as only Megan would do, she started talking about our plan. Full Steam Ahead Megan. (By this time, she had officially become the Chief Operating Officer, a title we would never give ourselves except for the fact that legally, on tax documents, we had to state our titles. We prefer titles like Chief Optimistic Officer or Chief Encouraging Officer, but the government doesn't offer those boxes to check.) We got off the phone, and about an hour later, she called me back with all the details of what our next steps should be. The show required a video submission, and she'd already written the answers to their questions.

"Do you want to practice now?" she asked me.

"Now?" I sputtered, still reeling at having been asked to audition. I looked around at my kitchen, the counter blanketed with the dirty pots and pans from last night's dinner, my open laptop on the table pinging with another new email to answer. Why do one-pot dinner recipes so rarely live up to their name?

"Yes," came my sister's sharp voice back over the line.

"Not really," I said with a laugh.

That wasn't good enough for my sister. If we were going to do this, we needed to know everything about our business's trajectory, inside and out. We couldn't be the least bit unprepared or unpolished. So for the next three months, along with our assigned *Shark Tank* producer, Megan led us in studying our answers, numbers, and pitch. Day after day, I'd pick up my ringing phone to hear my sister's voice on the other end.

"Do you have thirty?" Megan would ask. And for thirty minutes, we'd quiz each other on our business, ask the other to recite our pitch, and make sure there was no fumbling or we'd start all over again.

Then, the day of reckoning arrived. As we made our way out to Los Angeles to film our episode, she was the one with the paperwork, she was the one with the schedule, the one who rented a smart car, and also the one who'd planned a day of shopping, a Lakers game for us to attend, and dinner. She is the girl that *gets it done*, you guys. She makes it seem effortless, but if not for Megan's determination, organization, and persistence, you would have seen us appear much differently on national television. If I'm honest, I would have winged it. Yes, I would have winged it on national television.

This is what Megan does in every aspect of Tippi Toes: she makes it better. Often, I'll share an idea, dream, or goal, and she puts an action plan on paper with details, follow-up questions, and timelines. I'm the dreamer, while Megan helps me get it done -- a doer, if you will. The stuff that is less glamorous in my eyes, Megan takes time to lean into and learn so Tippi Toes benefits. Her response to me when I grumble and dread: "Just think: if we learn this now, we will know how to do it later."

My experience working with my family is that together, we are better! Together, we've grown faster, problem-solved quicker, and expanded our brand worldwide. Our dad is our director of worldwide merchandise, shipping our Tippi Toes gear around the world. You have never seen a box packaged so perfectly. We had to invest in packing tape because he would be danged if a box would prematurely open en route. Round and round he goes, making sure each box is secure. If we don't have a box to fit a specific package, he's the guy to make his own box. Meticulously, sizing the material and the cardboard. And Jennie, the oldest Lowery sister, although it took twenty-one years to get her to join our Tippi Toes family, now runs thriving Tippi Toes franchises in Nashville, Tennessee, and Cincinnati, Ohio. Our mom is still the helper to all, our cheerleader, the t-shirt counter, the box mover, the babysitter, the encourager, and the one who keeps the rest of us sane -- really simply put, she's the backbone for all of us.

Take action

Trust the belay

Who do you have in your life pushing you to be a better spouse, parent, or leader? I have learned over time that the people in our life help us carry our dreams as well as our burdens. Tippi Toes could not be where it is without the appearance of so many faces along the way, including the most familiar of faces: my family. Who in your life has helped you grow to be the person you are meant to be? What roles have they played in helping you?

What is a dream you can recognize that has become complete? For me, writing this book has been a huge dream. I'm in the middle of the process where you're reading right now, and it's not close to being done, but the hardest part, you guys, was *starting*. I didn't feel ready, didn't feel like I had enough to say, and fear crept in along with a whole bunch of doubt. I would put thoughts in my head like *Who on earth would want to read this? You are not a writer!* I began to convince myself I wasn't enough. This is when I leaned on those who saw more in me and believed I could be a bestseller. Bob Goff was a huge instrument for me in this process. While talking to the author on the phone, I unloaded all the self-doubting thoughts in my head, and his words back to me were simple and kind.

"I can't think of a book I would rather read more," he told me.

He is a *New York Times* best-selling author, and he just said that about *my* hypothetical book. He helped me define the "why" of penning my story, and I am certain without my "why" it would have been hard to press on. My why is to share Jesus with every person I meet. Writing a book and speaking allows me to do this on a larger scale. I hope to get my books in the hands of people I may never meet face to face so they can see how Jesus changed my life and carried my business, and I pray it helps them allow Jesus to enter their life in a real way as well. Then Bob helped me with the "how." Through his Dream Big Framework conference, he took me step by step through what I would need to do to reach my goal. He guided me and made what seemed like a mountain look more like a ton of small, manageable hills.

I remember sitting in a room with him, and as he was talking, he pulled out a belay. Not being a rock climber myself, I had never seen one or had any idea what it was used for. Bob explained that belays are used in rock climbing to secure the climber to something strong to hold them up so they don't fall. When I dug deeper into a belay device, Wikipedia describes how it acts as a friction brake so that when a climber falls with any slack in the rope, the fall is brought to a stop. Bob's words still ring in my ear today: "The trick to belaying is being tied to a solid rock. In our lives, the rock is the stuff that matters most. That's what we must be tied to."

For me, this moment was big. I want to be tied to initiatives that matter, missions that influence people. I believed in my heart God had a plan for me to write, but self-doubt flooded in. I would remind myself of my poor grades in school and how there were years of school records proving my potential to be otherwise. *Enough!* I said. I want to be held to the rock. That rock was Jesus, and I knew that being tied to Him, I could do anything, go anywhere, and impact the world in a great way. When I sputter or my path forward clouds over, I think back to belaying to Jesus, and that thought right there allows me to keep typing my book, keep growing Tippi Toes, keep speaking to audiences, keep living a life full of abundance so I can help impact the world for Jesus.

Gather your people, share with them your ultimate hope, and allow them to stretch out their hand to help you get there. God loves connection and partnership; think way back to Adam and Eve. We are meant to work together, be together, and glorify God through the gifts He has given us, *together.*

CHAPTER 5

You Plan, God Laughs (But Is Also

Really Proud of You)

Day by day, we get closer to that dream end goal we

have.

You have surely heard the phrase "Let's throw spaghetti against the wall and see what sticks." Well, when it comes to brainstorming, I happen to subscribe to it. God created me to be someone with all these ideas, and I can't sit on them. Picture a pot simmering on the stove right before the boiling point. Tiny bubbles race to the surface. If the pot sits on the burner long enough, the bubbles get bigger and sometimes boil over. That's me. Ideas percolating inside my heart. If I don't act on them -- and quickly -- I'm like a pot of water boiling over. But there are people, and maybe you're one of them, who sit and stew. And ruminate. And churn. Perhaps an idea has been smoldering for as long as you remember, and years later, there it still sits, burning a hole in your very soul.

When I speak at events about going after one's dreams, the very first question I ask is, "What do you want your life to look like?" Often, the very thing a person wants is only two to three months out if they would only *take action*. In 2019, I spoke at a business conference in Nashville. After the event, I was able to meet and greet some of the brilliant women in the audience. Many of them oozed with ideas for how to take their company to the next level. As I worked the room, a woman named Cora pulled me aside. I remembered her name because it was the same as my grandmother's. "I want to help my company implement an online portion of our business," she told me. "It would be cutting edge, and not one of our competitors does it yet. I just don't know where to start because I am not the owner of the company."

The first thing that came out of my mouth was, "Well done, Cora. You, my friend, are thinking in a way to advance your company and therefore become an asset to owners." I gave her my email address and told her I would love to follow up with her to help see what she could accomplish in her role. The first thing to note is she actually did email me. How often do we overlook an extended helping hand? She didn't just wish for help: she asked for it and then took me up on my offer. She and I exchanged emails, and for the next few weeks, we put together a plan to move her idea forward. Writing it down on paper with well-thought-out steps helped her see she was much closer to this dream being a reality than she thought. She checked in with me weekly, and we followed the steps we had laid out one by one until she was able to present her idea to her company. Today, her company has a way to increase sales that they didn't have before, all because she put a plan together and followed through. She was also rewarded for her "outside-the-box thinking," as her boss liked to call it, with a trip for her family to Disney World.

I learned the benefit of asking for help when, you guessed it, I was desperate. Early in my Tippi Toes days, I decided I wanted to host a recital. My first recital hit right at summertime, so costumes were easy: the kids would show up in their own swimsuits, and I purchased each of them some cheap sunglasses. The parents loved the show, and so did the kids. As winter rolled around, I wanted to give my dancers that same polished experience but got stuck on what they would wear. My dancers had been practicing dances that would fit a Western theme, so I wanted costumes to match. I considered having them all wear jeans and a white shirt, but that didn't fit the role of "dancer" very well. I kept thinking, and although I had zero experience in sewing, I thought I would give it a try and handmake 30 skirts for the girls to wear, and ask the boys to come in jeans. I would provide the bandanas for all. Most dance studios would order costumes and have parents pay for them, but I didn't take time to learn how that could happen and figured it would be simpler if I could just whip some up myself. So much easier said than done.

In my apartment, Chanda laughing right beside me, I threaded the little string into the needle hole, with blisters beginning to form on my fingertips. The idea in my head was grand, the real product a disaster. My bloody fingers were not up for this challenge. The lady in Hobby Lobby's fabric center made it sound so easy. After eight hours of trying, gluing, and struggling, I had to run and teach a class at the Guest Inn hotel on Main Street in Norman. That's right, my second semester with Tippi Toes, I asked a cheap hotel if I could rent a conference room for parents to bring their kids in to dance with me. The smell of smoke as you entered didn't turn anyone away, and I had a core group of five families with a dozen kids between them who supported this idea.

At the end of the class, I playfully joked I would need to get back to trying to make these costumes. One of the moms piped up and asked how I was doing it. After I dodged her question with comments on how well her daughters were dancing, she asked again. I admitted I was struggling and really needed some help. "Hey Michelle," I said offhand, "any chance you know how to sew?". But her eyes lit up! You know that look you're returned when you inadvertently ask someone about their sweet spot? This was that moment. Michelle went on and on about her sewing machine and all the projects she had sewn. Seeing my opportunity, I made a quick proposal to her: "How about I don't charge you for classes for the rest of the semester, and you help me finish these costumes?" She was in and so was I. I asked for help, Michelle said yes, and we had the cutest little Western dancers at our performance. She and I continued this bartering relationship for a few years until I started to purchase costumes from a costume company.

Most business owners don't dream of setting up an LLC and a small business bank account, signing contracts, and researching locations. That's the drudgery. For me, I dreamt of pink recital tutus and a group of kids dancing with big grins on their faces! However, the plodding must be done, and it's important not to be overwhelmed by the details. Sometimes that looks like boring meetings, rejection, and cleaning toilets. Other times, you get one letter from the state saying you're delinquent in filing your business license and another from the IRS stating you owe taxes. Did I want to hide under the covers and have those letters and their tough directives vanish? You bet. Yet these are all necessary tasks to take a business owner to his or her endpoint.

Seeing my clear goals written out reminded me of the purpose behind all these chores. If I wanted Tippi Toes to continue, I would need to perform the less glamorous tasks to keep my business afloat. Taking myself seriously while I took these small steps to keep my business in good standing meant it felt like there was movement with Tippi Toes even when from the outside, not much appeared to be happening. There were times for me, like I'm sure there have been for you, when I worked so hard and didn't see a single positive result. Zilch. Not a one. But that's precisely when having clear goals matters. When you write them down, it is harder to throw in the towel when the going gets tough.

Planning has been key for my personal life and allows my business life to thrive. When I can take care of my tasks by crossing each item off that trusty to-do list, it clears my head and helps me be a better wife and mom. I swear I am a nicer person when my house is clean; come on, can any of you relate? Most days, I have habits in place so my day flows and by the time my kids are home from school, I can be all in with them.

A big part of that is I generally get up and work out at 6 a.m. so I can start the day high on endorphins. I've of course made a career on the benefit of movement for one's physical health, but I can't stress enough how exercising is good for the mind, too. I'm able to think more clearly, prioritize my to-do list, and kick the day's booty. My guess is you could use a little dance in your life, too.

Take action

Reflect on your path

So what is it for you? In the next twelve months, what do you want to be true about yourself, your family, and your business? Spend time reflecting on this. If you want to see real life change, it takes knowing what it is you are going for and then developing a focused plan to get there. I like to list four personal goals and four family goals to narrow my focus, like this:

Sarah's personal goals:

1. Keep my heart and mind open to God's direction for my life

2. Spend quality time with my family

3. Eat clean food and work out daily to fuel my body

4. Be encouraging to every single person I meet

Sarah's business goals:

1. Expand Tippi Toes to more countries

2. Write another book

3. Work closely with our Tippi Toes franchise owners

4. Travel the world with my family while speaking at events

Being diligent in *both* personal and business goals aids one another. If we just focus on the personal, we feel defeated in business. When we just focus on business, we run ourselves ragged and are not personally fulfilled. We must be balanced and feel in control in both areas to feel and see sustainable success.

Now it's your turn:

Personal goals:

1.

2.

3.

4.

Business goals:

1.

2.

3.

4.

Next, I ask myself some questions to make sure what I'm wanting will push me to be the best version of myself.

When I complete these goals, I will feel:

What is the purpose of reaching these goals?

Who will reaching these goals impact and how?

When I get stuck or have a task that I don't understand, I will:

Go back to your goals and add how long each goal will realistically take you if you use the method of daily deposits, which we talked about in Chapter 1. If this part feels strange to you, let me help you. Think about my friend Cora. She wasn't able to move her idea into action until she was told to put a plan together, expected to do so by her mentor (that's me!). From my view, it was a simple conversation, but for her, I moved a mountain. Sometimes we just have to get out of our own way. Stop telling yourself all the reasons it won't work, and put a timeline to your dream.

I want to pretend you and I are sitting at a coffee shop. (You pick the spot; I don't drink coffee but don't want to miss this time with you.) We sit down, and you start telling me about this idea you have. Here, take time to tell me about it. All the details and facets of this dream.

I respond, "That really sounds amazing. So why haven't you done it yet?"

Now share all the things that have stood in your way and why you haven't moved forward.

So if you were to take action today, what are the first few things you would need to do? Give me just three tasks that have been holding you back, those three to-do list items that have you groaning and reaching for your phone, the remote, your insert-custom-distraction-here. If you don't know what to do first, who would you reach out to that could help you?

I have found with Tippi Toes that our goals and dreams continue to grow and change. Had I said the first day when I walked into the very first daycare that I wanted to have an international franchise, that would have been amazing. However, in that moment at that time, I didn't nearly have a way to make that a reality. Not even close. No groundwork had been laid yet. It's so easy to want to jump to the final, biggest idea we have and then get frustrated when we aren't as far along as we think we should be. So let's just practice taking the first step, then the next and the next, and day by day, we get closer to that dream end goal we have.

CHAPTER 6

Wake Up, Joseph!

What blessings are you sleeping through?

When my sweet little four-year-old, Hank, was in preschool, he desperately wanted to play Jesus's dad in the annual Christmas play. For weeks before he and his classmates performed for their families, they worked to learn eight songs that would be part of the program. Teachers and parents made all the costumes so each student looked just right for their part. My daughter Lucy, being our oldest, brought our first experience with the play. Lucy's outfit was simple but cute: she wore a white sweatsuit with a little black dot on the tip of her nose and a headband with oversized wool sheep ears attached. When Lucy took the stage in the back center, she sang her little heart out, and, as only Lucy can do, she shined and smiled the entire time.

Then there was our next oldest, Lola. This girl loves to sing, so her main focus was making sure she got all the words right rather than playing a specific part. She played an angel in the end, wearing a halo in her short hair. Her fair skin made her blue eyes sparkle. Lola, as a young girl, was normally shy in front of adults, so she always made sure she was prepared for what she had to do and, boy, was she. She sang every single word to the songs like she was the only one on stage.

As Hank and I reminisced about his sisters' past Christmas plays, he told me he knew what he wanted to be for his turn in the big play.

"Mom, I really want to be either Jesus or Joseph," Hank said.

He continued to talk about his quest to play one of the leads for the next few weeks. I gently explained there are lots of important roles in the birth of Jesus he may have forgotten about. I reminded him about the donkey, cattle, wise men, and even the shepherd. And he agreed all those parts were cool -- but that didn't change his resolve to be cast as either Jesus or Joseph. I'm fairly certain he dropped some pretty heavy hints to his teachers to make sure he would get one of his choice roles. I walked in to pick him up from school one Monday, and he ran to me with a huge smile.

"Hank has some exciting news to share with you," his teacher said.

He hugged me with a big, awesome Hank hug.

"I'm Joseph!" he shouted.

Hank's smile shone brighter than our Christmas tree at midnight. The walk from his classroom to the car was pretty long, and we talked nonstop the whole way. The main thing he kept mentioning was how he was the one who got to be the closest to baby Jesus. He reassured me that they would use a baby doll, but he was so proud he would get to watch "Jesus" all during the show. The other big win was how he'd get to sit in a chair with Mary while all the other kids in his class would stand behind them. When the girls got home from school, this was the first piece of news he shared with them.

"Hank, that is the best part!" Lucy cheered for her little brother. We celebrated with a dance party in our kitchen.

The day of the show, I picked up Hank from school for his usual 1 p.m. departure time. We went home, had lunch, and waited for the girls and Adam to get home from school and work. We had to arrive back at school at 5:15 to get ready for the 6 p.m. show. Hank rarely napped at this age, and he was so excited for his show, there was no way I was going to get him to rest. Hank wore his button-up shirt and nice dress pants and made sure to comb his hair so he was stage-ready. On the way to the play, we all sang Christmas carols. When our family arrived at the school, we dropped him off in his classroom so he could prepare for the show. Hank was so excited and happily ran into the room with the other students. The rest of our family took our seats, and it wasn't long before the house lights went down. It was almost time for the Christmas show to start.

The lights hit the front of the stage, and Hank's class took their places. A wooden manger sat in the center of the church altar, with straw where baby Jesus lay, right between Hank and the girl playing Mary. The children filled the altar: a bunch of sheep, cows, donkeys, a few angels, and three wise men with Mary and Joseph. The children sang at the top of their lungs, and you could tell from listening they had been practicing for weeks. Then the narration of the story began. As the narrator began explaining the story of Jesus and His birth, I looked over at my son and noticed him blinking more than usual.

"Is Hank supposed to be doing that?" Adam whispered.

As a mom, I went to worry first. *Is he okay? Is he about to pass out?*

"Do you think he has something in his eye?" I whispered back to Adam.

His blinks started to get a lot longer, and he looked like something might be medically wrong. The next song started, and the children sang loudly while Hank's blinks grew slower and slower. His head began to droop and his shoulders went down in his chair. The children were all singing, but Hank had quit.

I looked over at Adam, frantic. "Do you think he's okay? Do you think he's getting sick? What's going on?"

And as soon as the words came out of my mouth, Hank's head hit his lap. He had fallen asleep on the stage.

I sat there not knowing what to do. *Surely he'll wake up*, I thought to myself. And sure enough, as the next song started, Hank's eyes came open. But they quickly closed again, and this time his head flung backwards, hitting the kid behind him. All the kids around him continued singing for five more songs. Hank began a routine of waking up, singing a little, and then falling right back to sleep. Eventually, the long blinks just quit, and Hank was out cold. My sweet little Joseph, who had been so excited about his part in the play, was completely asleep in front of a crowd of probably 100 people watching and laughing hysterically that Joseph had fallen asleep during the biggest part of the play.

We have all been guilty of sleeping through some of life's greatest moments, not appreciating their glory. It might be that guy you fell in love with and hoped he would propose; now married to him, you nag him over insignificant faults. Or those children you prayed for so intently, but instead of engaging with them, you are hustling through a busy schedule just trying to get to the next task and not enjoying the current moment. Maybe the job you so badly wanted you now dread waking up to commute to. All these moments, we can be caught asleep. Today is the day to wake up, acknowledge your blessings, and move into a place of growth.

To live a life with purpose, you must be intentional with how you spend your time. Each day is a day you don't get back, and to live it fully engaged will allow you to access your deep purpose. Thinking back to Bob Goff asking me "why," defining my inspiration shaped my days so they became much more purposeful. I want to share Jesus with the world. I can't do that being inactive, dormant, sedentary. I must fully engage with my life's purpose and those people around me. Before I defined my why, I may have been considered on autopilot while running Tippi Toes, slowly growing it while caring for those around me. It was good, it was nice, but I wasn't tapping into all I was capable of. To do this, run at a dead sprint wherever you are, tap into your heart's desires, and keep digging until you want to jump up in the air and click your heels because you know you are in that sweet spot. When what you are doing allows you to connect with your why and make that ambition come to life, you, my friend, are living fully engaged.

When our lives are driven by our why, it isn't exhausting; it is exhilarating. I challenge you to find your why and be fully engaged. Hank badly wanted to be Joseph, but it wasn't because he wanted to own that role and allow the audience to see what a dedicated father Joseph was. No, his 4-year-old mind wanted that chair next to Mary so he didn't have to stand the entire play -- and could apparently rest peacefully during the show. Don't do this like Hank did. Know your why, believe in your purpose, and decide to engage in this one life God has given you. Your family, your career, your passion, your people. You have a choice. You could sleep. You could be on autopilot. Or you can be *fully engaged*. The difference lies in your habits, your thoughts, and accounting for your time.

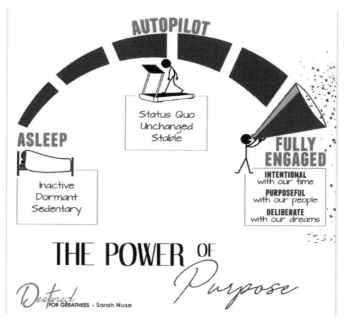

In the middle of the Power of Purpose graphic, you see *autopilot*. This word is often associated with "going through the motions." We can busy ourselves with all the activity supporting our dream without ever actually touching the dream. For example, you can buy all the books on how to fix a car, but until you get under the hood yourself, you will not actually repair that car. For me, I could have bought a book on how to start a business. I could have told myself I was working on the step-by-step process to build my business by reading this book or that book. I know better. It took me making *a darn cold call* to get the motor running.

The arrival point of the Power of Purpose is to be engaged at full throttle. We take account of our time. We can measure our progress. We schedule deep and meaningful moments with our families. We propel our dreams forward without distraction. We demand daily habits of ourselves, never getting out of sync with our dreams. Our thoughts never venture outside the language it will take to get us there: *I can and I will!*

So, what is it that you want? Are you passionately chasing after something important to you? As we run after the next dream important to us, we must stay awake and alert. Sometimes it takes effort. I know that when I am at a business conference, I'm amped up just talking business with like-minded people. Often, the last thing I want to do is sign up for the conference, but once I'm there, I am so happy I did it. Can you relate? It takes stepping out a little and saying yes to the right things. It's recognizing where we are during our journey without cruising over to autopilot.

I believe our instincts are a gift from God. When we have a thought that won't go away, when there is good behind it, God is steering our lives, and we must listen to the voice directing us. When I have done this in my life, I can feel God guiding me in a direction I could never find by myself. This book right here is a perfect example of just saying yes to God. I could sit and tell you all the reasons I don't believe I am a writer, but God doesn't see it that way. The more I've been writing, the more I have sensed God asking me to write more, carve out more time for this project, prompt me with fresh ideas. I have had dreams about this book, visions of people reading it, and I sense God all over it. It's gotten me out of bed in the middle of the night or early in the morning, while my family still sleeps soundly, to sit at my desk passionately tapping away on my keyboard, flooded with thoughts to share. When I start going down the road of self-doubt (come on, we all do it, right?), I stop and say, "God, if this is what you want me to do, give me words to write and the people to help me make it happen." What I receive from Him is a clear yes to me. Opportunities open up, relationships are built, and the direction of my life seems crystal clear.

We must be alert, stay in tune to these nudges, and, for goodness' sake, stay awake! For me with Tippi Toes, I know I must keep up with the current music, trends for kids, and the latest business books. When I let my learning languish, Tippi Toes stops growing -- and so do I. Growing is constantly practicing what I learn, having real life experiences, continuing to read, have conversations, and build knowledge to share with others. My friend and fellow entrepreneur Pam Shaw created a workbook called *Designing My Life: Breakthrough Goal Setting*. In it, she asks 140 pages worth of questions to help the reader squeeze the most out of their life and their potential. My favorite part of her book is about patterns. She writes, "If you don't intentionally change, alter, or shift the direction of your life, it will continually migrate in the same direction." This is essentially being asleep, never ruffling the pattern that will bring you results.

Take action

Stay alert

Below are prompts to help us look forward and take those small, daily steps to our dreams to remain vigilant and shift our direction to one aimed at attainment. For me, when I was trying to reach that 50-student goal Adam had set up on my bathroom mirror, it looked something like this:

Big goal: Make enough money to pay my car payment

First action step: Ask the local daycare (in person!) if I can teach dance

Daily: Map out other schools that might allow me to come teach

Weekly: Spend every moment of free time driving around Norman, Oklahoma, giving my sales pitch

Monthly: Sign up at least 20 new students per month

Now it's your turn:

Big goal:

First action step:

Daily:

Weekly:

Monthly:

I don't want a day to go by where I don't celebrate the life I have right now, the family I was brought up in, the husband I was so fortunate to marry, the kids I have the privilege of raising, and the business with which I am entrusted. I can't afford to be sound asleep; it's too expensive to my soul to miss this. I want to find joy in the life I have been given -- so I do. I color a large piece of butcher paper with "I love you" signs and hang them in the garage so when the door goes up, my family is welcomed home. I hide candy in my kids' shoes so when they put them on, it's one more reminder of how much they are loved. On a whim, I'll pick up gas station Icees before waiting in the afternoon carpool line, anticipating my kids' excitement at the unexpected treat. It can be Monday or Thursday, it doesn't matter, because we need to be fully engaged all days. So friends, let's celebrate! Let's embrace the hard, the sticky, the fun, the exciting, the unexpected -- but let's make sure we just don't fall asleep and miss all these beautiful moments that are molding us into who are supposed to be.

CHAPTER 7

Experts

Not all mentors are created equally.

I have spent my entire life studying two experts in a dicey area: marriage. My mom and dad are the best role models I know when it comes to love. I grew up listening to the sound of a good marriage: the constant patter of Dad's adoring words about my mom sprinkled into conversation. "I-love-you-isn't-Sallie-the-greatest-she-did-an-awesome-job." No periods. No long pauses. A rhythm with no end. It *could* have been different: he *could* have picked apart every tiny thing she did that he didn't like. Some marriages are like that. But I know I am lucky to have been set up in my life to love big. My parents hold hands, still, at the age of 70. My dad can be seen pinching my mom's behind as he walks by her in the kitchen, proclaiming that Sallie is the love of his life.

The walls of our home were built from the devoted words my dad laid out daily to my mom. He taught us that loving your spouse is an act of benevolence. And Mom's relentless pursuit of family togetherness bonded us to this day, when we remain unbreakable by age or distance. What I witnessed as a child was each parent doing everything they could to enhance their spouse's life. True love, the kind of love that keeps a couple together for a lifetime, is not a feeling but an attitude. They both continue that attitude after 43 years together, and I continue to take notes. So, yeah, I know a pair of experts.

My marriage is the highest-value relationship in my life. Long before Adam and I married, I dreamed of being his wife. We dated for four years during college. He had a level head about finishing school before we tied the knot, but me, not so much. I wanted to marry him a few days after meeting him, really. *Days*. I recognized early on that he was my person. My entire life, I had seen the joy my parents received from being married. All the mental notes I took when I was younger were filed away, and with Adam, I was ready to put the lessons into practice. Being married to Adam now for 17 years, I realize my parents' marriage was a gift of an example. I see things I do now with Adam that I got from watching and studying my parents.

Sitting in the living room, my sisters and I would be glued to *Saved by the Bell* while Mom fixed dinner. When we would hear the garage door go up, that was our cue: the TV went off, and we all ran to the door to greet Dad. My mom wanted everyone to immediately feel welcome in our home, especially our dad. Today, if you come into our home, my children are expected to greet visitors at the front door, walk them to the door when they leave, and, most importantly, we all run to the garage door to welcome Adam home from his day. From date nights to one-on-one nighttime chats to grossing us out by kissing in the kitchen, my parents put each other first. It gave us kids security knowing the two of them were deeply in love. The reasons mentors are powerful is they have been where we want to go or done what we desire to do.

When you have a passion or want to get better in a specific area, it is wise to look for a mentor who can guide you and share past experiences to help you put your best foot forward. A few years ago, Adam and I were so excited to take the kids skiing in Banff, Alberta. We had really enjoyed skiing early in our marriage, but since having kids, we hadn't made time for it. Lucy was nine, Lola eight, and Hank six, and we thought they were the perfect ages to enjoy this activity. The cold mountain air whipped against our thick snow gear as we snapped those pesky boots on our feet and walked with a bend in our knees to make it to the mountain. Ski school was a must so the kids could learn before they went out on their own. I gave the kids a quick rundown of my limited ski knowledge. If you have taken your kids skiing, you may remember your first time, and I wonder if it was like ours. We had such high hopes, but before the kids even got to their lesson, they were *done*. They wanted to head back to the warm hotel, build a fire, toast marshmallows, and play games. They were done walking in boots, done being cold, and done trying to figure out how to navigate the mountain. We dropped them off at ski school with two of them in tears and the third also unhappy. I'll admit, we did a drop-and-run. We got to the top of the mountain to go on as many runs of our own as we could before pickup time; that's what good parents do, right?

As we finished up our own day of skiing and the kids' lessons were about to end, we made our way to the pickup area. When we got there, Lucy, Lola, and Hank were each shuffling their feet around in a circle holding onto what looked like a broom. They weren't on the mountain. They weren't even on a hill. They had not moved from the spot from where we dropped them off, six hours earlier.

The instructor nodded at me. "Good day," he said, giving a thumbs up.

The kids were less than thrilled that they never made it to the mountain. Adam and I looked at each other and said, "Let's go!" *Surely the kids can handle this*, we thought. We took them to a small portion of a hill so they could show off the skills they'd learned that day. But, skills? What skills? They would have been better off with us teaching them because they'd learned *zilch*. I quickly realized this wasn't the best idea. The kids rode the magic carpet up the bunny slope, and all three barreled on top of each other. Skis facing the sun, butts in the snow. After a little help, they moved. Hank's face looked miserable as someone cut him off and he plowed into the back of them. Lola was slow and steady but confident, and made it down the hill without interruption. Lucy was like stop-and-go traffic. She had the pizza pie shape with her skis down perfectly, but it seemed like that was really the only gear she knew. Adam and I were puzzled about why they didn't catch on during their lesson. Then we learned other families on the trip with us had the same feeling about their kids, so we hatched a plan to hit a different mountain the next day. On the way back to the hotel, we asked the kids what they had learned.

"Welp, guys, not a darn thing," Lola said in her sarcastic, funny way. "We only learned how to make pizza with our feet."

Lucy chimed in. "I don't think our coach liked his job," she said.

A full day of skiing would typically wear you out, but with our kids' lack of skiing that day, they were anxious to get up early the next morning to try a new mountain. Adam and I were thankful they were still determined to learn, though. We headed toward Lake Louise for the day. As we got out of our car, we saw the coolest setup where kids could ski. There were colored flags signifying different groups everywhere, kids cruising down the mountain with instructors close behind, and kids laughing, playing, and dominating the mountain. The bunny slope looked like a real mountain with a magic carpet lining the side. As we moved to ask about lessons, the instructor who'd been teaching 6 to 10 year olds came over to chat with our kids. He asked them what they hoped to learn, what they already knew, and what they feared on the mountain. He was engaged with them, and we learned he had been awarded many ski instruction awards over his twenty years on this mountain. I was thrilled. Since the kids had already had a full day of lessons the day before, we opted for a three-hour lesson in hopes this would give them the confidence to go up the mountain with us.

Experts are so interested in their skill or craft that their excitement rubs off on others, too. It did for us: this instructor had our kids completely occupied with his storytelling, his Australian accent, and his passion for skiing. Three hours later, Adam and I dropped in at ski school to see all three of our kids cruising up and down the mountain without falls, frustrations, or fears. They were grinning from ear to ear and yelling for us to watch them. I could happily say at this point our kids could ski.

It took someone who knew more than we did to help them better than we could. What stood out most, though, is he was fully engaged while living his dream of instructing on one of the best mountains in Canada. Our kids could have continued trying to learn from the same mountain instructor they had the day before. Eventually, they would have either understood the sport of skiing or been so frustrated they quit. But by finding the right expert, all three learned how to ski and felt confident in their abilities.

We have to be intentional about whom we are seeking advice from and how they can come along with us to reach our dreams and goals. Find the people who will keep you aware and keep you in tune with what God has called you to do. Get a few experts in your court to help you move from an idea to living out your potential. Be alert in knowing what you need. We need ideas with action, not ideas with only excitement. Also, be the expert for someone else and help them find their way using lessons you've learned yourself.

In 2017, I was fortunate enough to be at a speaking event with a member of the Chick-fil-A corporate team, and he took the opportunity to embody that role for me.

We got to talking backstage, and he asked who my business mentor was. I answered as best I could, tap dancing around a less sheepish way of admitting I didn't have one, when he said, "Hey, I would love to introduce you to some of our executive women who I think would be delighted to mentor you as you continue to build Tippi Toes." Jackpot! Although Chick-fil-A is fast food and we dance, we both have the same goal: to serve others. Their team at the event wanted to make connections, and they did it to the fullest. They invited our Tippi Toes leaders to come and spend a day with their franchising team to learn how they select their best operators, and they shared in detail how their company started and the hurdles they work through as a business. They served us from the minute we walked through the doors. My favorite part about meeting Brandon and the team from Chick-fil-A is he said, "Our door is always open. We want to continue to help you grow." Chick-fil-A has had an incredible influence on me, and no, not just because of the famously delicious Chick-fil-A sauce. I admire the way they handle customers and business, in general. They don't see their success as a secret sauce; they have a servanthood mentality and are doing everything they can to help others.

Since this time, Tippi Toes has worked to adopt this model, starting a program for our teachers to become owners by taking certain business preparation classes with us. We also have opened our Tippi Toes conference normally just for the owners of franchises to all owners, staff and teachers involved in Tippi Toes. Until our relationship with Chick-fil-A, we were so secretive, only allowing owners to attend these conferences. The truth is that the more we opened our company to our dance teachers, the greater the connection became and the more they could witness and engage with the heart of Tippi Toes. It was a win-win and has helped develop our business model significantly.

Take action

Look for your mentors

Experts are defined as a person who has a comprehensive and authoritative knowledge of a skill in a particular area. Malcolm Gladwell shared in his bestselling book *Outliers* that to become an expert it takes 10,000 hours (or approximately ten years) of *deliberate practice* to become an expert. To break this down even further, the word "deliberate" means to carefully think or talk something through, slow and measured, the pace of this kind of careful decision making. "Practice" means to repeatedly or regularly perform an activity or exercise a skill in order to improve or maintain one's proficiency. This isn't just 10,000 hours of doing something. It is 10,000 hours of carefully thinking through something with careful decision making and practicing regularly overtime.

You may feel stuck and know you need a mentor but don't know what kind of specialist you need. Here's how I've sectioned out the experts in specific areas of my life:

1. My parents (marriage and parenting)

2. My pastor (pointing me toward Jesus)

3. Bob Goff (speaking/dreaming big)

4. Reid and Reese Ryan (brothers and business experts)

5. Nutrition coaches (health and exercise)

Is there a skill you are wanting to learn? An idea you want to turn into a business? A mission where you want to help? A product you want to launch? Or maybe it feels like a little bit of all of this. So let's break it down:

Do you know someone who has done something like what you are wanting to do? If yes, put them on your list. For example, say a new restaurant opened in your town, and you've long been finessing the menu of your own future fantasy eatery. You don't know the owner but reach out to meet with her and learn from her experience.

How about digging deeper? Let's say you really want to learn how to (you fill in the blank). Think first: *this person* does it best, next *this person* does it great, and I know someone who knows them, then *this person* has done what I want to do, and maybe they aren't totally thriving yet, but they're further than I am.

Now, how can you get in contact with one of the three?

Let's say your first pick is the best of the best, and you really want to connect with them. Here are a few ways I have found to be helpful: first, go to their website to learn about the products or programs they sell specifically in the area you want to grow. Look to see if there is a point of contact where you can email, direct message, or mail a letter asking for help. Next, find people in their circle from whom they learned. If you can't get in contact with the expert you dream of, possibly you can connect with someone who taught them. Sift through all your contact options and break them down one by one. If you hit a brick wall, go to your next option. The more you search, the more you will find a slew of people willing to help you grow.

Experts in your life and areas in which they can help:

1.

2.

3.

4.

5.

When we're starting something new, there is so much to learn that it can be hard to know where to start. If this is true for you, let's start with what you can do *right now*, this instant. When I started Tippi Toes, I knew I could make marketing materials, create content for my classes, and spend time looking up locations to pitch my idea to. So I started there. Having a way to advertise my established dance routines at brick-and-mortar locations helped me build confidence that what I was doing was going to work.

So what would that be for you? Think of three or four concrete tasks to help get you started. Start with where you already excel. Next, think of what you can do to move forward -- those small, daily deposits again. You may be lacking in resources, meaning knowledge, supplies, or funds. Let's take this book, for example. I can write. However, my resources were limited. When it came to how to get a book from my mind to a bookstore, I was at a loss. I can't edit, design, publish, or mass distribute. This could be a problem for someone like me who wants to impact the WORLD. The world is a large place, and I am just one person. So how does this happen? I have to start thinking *how I can accomplish this goal, what* my *contribution toward the dream can be right now.* Guess what I did? I started by writing. I know that sounds so simple, but often we try to make it harder than it is. To get a book out, writing must happen first. What is your first step? Is it something you can do today? Yes! Today!

As I finished my writing, I made a post on social media. "I wrote a book, and now I am looking for an editor. Does anyone have any recommendations?" Sound scary? It was for me, but I didn't want to waste any time. Speaking our goals out loud is powerful. It allows other people in on what you are doing and holds you accountable to what you said you are going to do. Look what happened next: my friend Autumn commented on my post, tagging her friend Emily, who is an editor. Connection was made! It was big. Emily and I talked, and she immediately understood my goals for my book and began to help stretch my stories into conversations. The more details she asked for, the more the stories would come alive. She helped me think as a writer in a way I had never thought before. For months, we exchanged emails back and forth. She was like a detailed pen pal, digging into my very soul. I came to love the writing process and the way she helped me develop my stories.

Could it be possible that today, with all of technology's possibilities, you are only one ask away from putting your dream in motion? I dare you to try it. Type your words into that little box, and hit "Post." You never know someone may be on the other side of the computer with the exact skill set you need. It's the one step in front of the next that gives the idea momentum to continue moving forward. I could have written my book and then sat on it. I could have tucked it away in a hope chest, sit in the space of telling myself I could never impact anyone, or I could maybe just maybe take a chance on myself, dream big and go after what God put inside my heart. What if you don't take your chance and go for your dream, connecting the dots to make your dream happen. You will be robbing others of the greatness inside of you. The greatness that God is wanting to get out into the world. I believe it is our job to listen to that still, small voice that nudges us forward. That prompt, that excitement that says *I can and I will.* It is your duty to keep stepping forward, connecting the dots, and shutting out self-doubt. Give yourself an opportunity to live the life you have imagined.

CHAPTER 8

Warm-Up Girl

Give them hell, Bear.

My freshman year of high school, I got it in my head that I wanted to try out for our school's tennis team. Unlike most of my friends, my backstory did not include tennis. I didn't know a backspin from a cross-court shot. It's fair to say I had some work to do, so I began taking lessons and developed an insane addiction to the sport. It was all I wanted to do in my free time, and any chance I could get, I would take a lesson, play in a tournament, or just hit against my garage door, working to keep getting better.

There were only seven spots open on the tennis team. Six would actually get to play, and the seventh was the alternate. A simple tournament would shake out where each girl ranked, and I wanted one of the six spots to be mine. My final match during tryouts was against a girl I felt I could beat, Leah. We split sets, meaning she won the first group of games and I won the second. After battling for two hours on the court for that last team spot, we were both exhausted, fighting hard for that number six position. It was my serve. I tossed the ball up and smacked it over the net. She returned the ball, and it nicked the net. For half a second, that point was mine, until it wasn't. The ball nicked the tape then rolled down the net on my side. It was unreachable. That point, the one that was mine, made her number six. The match was hers. I became the seventh girl, the alternate, the runner-up. In my mind, the loser.

Disappointment stung my eyes, but I congratulated her with a smile. The long walk to our respective cars felt lonely to me. It was just us: the winner, the loser, and our parents. Not a soul said a word; what could they say? Leah was understandably excited to have just made the team while I was crushed. My dad tossed my bag in the trunk with a thud. As I climbed into the car and shut the door, my mom reached back and smiled, just in time for me to start wailing. When my dad got behind the wheel, I heard him say, "Give them hell, Bear." I thought to myself, *Sure felt like I just did.* I wiped a mixture of sweat and tears from my cheeks as he spoke again. "I mean it, Bear, give them hell." Perplexed, I leaned in to listen to the pep talk I so badly needed.

"Bear," he said, "this is your shot. You have the opportunity to push these girls harder than they have ever been pushed by being the best you can be. Number seven is one spot away from the team. Make these girls earn their positions all year long. Be their biggest cheerleader when they are playing, but let them know you are coming for a position on this team. Fight, Bear, fight hard, if this is something you want. Just because it didn't happen today doesn't mean it isn't going to happen. God has a plan. He gave you drive and a solid work ethic. Lean into what you missed this match, and grow from it."

I memorized my dad's words, which lit a fire beneath me. His pep talk gave me motivation to push, grow, and work. Within minutes of stepping off the court in devastation, my sorrow turned into determination, and I couldn't wait to get back on the court the next day. Do you need to hear my dad's words, too? Insert your nickname here: "____, this is your shot. Fight, ___, fight hard." Words, oh how words have power. My parents so easily might have told me "good try" and patted me on the back, but they didn't. They called out my fight. Just because something doesn't work out the way we want or plan doesn't mean it isn't part of the growth process. Immediately, I replaced how I saw myself before with believing myself to be an integral part of the team: number seven with a new attitude! My job was to make my team better. Coach Schmitz and each girl on the team knew how I desired one of the top six spots, so each time I played them, I would go as hard as possible. They got better, I got better, we all got better -- now *that* is teamwork. Although I wasn't on the court as much as I wanted to be, I became part of a team that was going places. When we traveled to tournaments, I analyzed other players. I observed the mannerisms of the great competitors and the sore losers. I studied ball placement, the high fives the doubles players would give each other, and trick serves. I would listen to different coaches yell across the court and see how the singles players ran their competitors to enfeeblement. I used each moment to listen and learn, knowing that when my time came, I would be ready.

It was May. All seven of us girls were excited for the week to come, which would get us closer to the state tournament. Our team loaded up on the buses to head to Oklahoma City from Tulsa. We braided each other's hair in small sections, a bunch of freshmen girls giddy at getting to skip a few days of school. Day after day, win after win, our team made the headlines: "Freshmen Girls Shocking the Tennis World." "The Unbeatable Freshmen." And guess what? We did it, as a team. We won! We were crowned the 1996 tennis champions. Although I wasn't on the court, I was a vital, instrumental part of the team. I warmed up each girl before her match, ran to refill water, kept our coach up to date on scores, or rebraided my teammates' hair. I was a true member of this team. I believed it, and so did every single person who knew I was on the team. Nobody asked which role I played because when you are part of a team, you work together as one. One person's defeat is all of ours, and one victory is ours to share as well. Never in the history of the number seven has there been a better seven; I can promise you that.

Building a team requires you to take on positions that seem unglamorous. What I learned through this experience is my position was no less significant when I was number seven than when I was number six the next year. Yes, when I was on the court, there was a lot left up to me. However, I could not have performed the way I did without the team that was in place. It took me pushing hard, fighting for my position, to make my teammates better and fight to keep their own positions.

I continued to work on my tennis game that first year on the team, and after almost getting to have one of the six coveted positions, I knew more than ever I wanted to be on that court the following year. I found a drive in myself to move my position from warm-up girl to the on-the-court girl. I wanted it so badly that it's all I thought about -- which is saying a lot for a high schooler, who has everything on the brain all the time. I signed up for more lessons and tournaments and would drill almost every day after school. I had my eyes laser-focused on being one of the six on the court.

The next year's tryouts came, and by the skin of my teeth, I landed on the team as the sixth player. This meant that the fifth player and I would be doubles partners. We played hard and worked day in and day out to get better. By junior year, I finally had a secured regular spot on the tennis team, no tryouts this time. A new girl landed on the team, and we were paired as partners. We really were meant to be partners because we complemented one another, pushed each other to get better, and hustled every minute on the court. She and I were seeded #2 in the state tournament. As we did in years past, we braided our hair, told funny stories, and walked in the tennis complex with excitement and anticipation for the week's tournament.

Day after day, win after win, our team was the headline: "Junior Girls Back for Victory," "The Unbeatable Freshman are Now Juniors." We kept adding points to our team total and our final score. The last day of the tournament, my partner and I were in the finals. It was late, the air had begun to cool, and the lights on the court reflected off our rackets. The way this tournament worked made this the most important match of my life: if we won this doubles match, it would mean we would be individual state champions, but more importantly, it would give our team enough points to become the team champions like we had two years ago, when I was player #7. My partner and I were focused, and the crowd was engaged and loud. It was time. Going into three sets, I hear from the top of the hill in a loud, boisterous voice, "Give them hell, Bear." With that cheer from my dad, I returned a serve with my backhand down the line, and that point made our team the 1998 state champions in Oklahoma. The girls from Bishop Kelley had done it again. This time, I was on the court and a vital, instrumental part of the team. My role looked different than it had in years past, but the outcome was the exact same: champions.

Sometimes building a team takes you being the "warm-up girl," while other times, it's being the "on-the-court girl" that pushes your team over the edge for the ultimate victory. Today when I look back at tennis, what I most remember is that we won state in 1996 and 1998 as a team. I remember our braids, the funny stories, and the moments we cried because we were overwhelmed by what we had accomplished. We. When building a team, we can't think of the word "I." It is all about surrounding yourself with people who will push you to be the best, people who are so good at what they do that to reach their level, you must push yourself to be even better. Being part of a team means seeing the goals and missions of those around you and all running in the same direction. If you are in a leadership role, and I suspect you are or at least want to be if you are reading this, you have the opportunity to build a team and occupy a unique role within that group. You are a mom or a dad building a family. You are a business owner helping your company grow. You are part of a family, part of a church, part of a sports team, part of an online community. Each of us is meant to help build and help one another grow. Building a team, no matter in what capacity, takes a special person. I have seen how the best leaders are the ones who allow everyone else to shine. They are the ones who are constantly encouraging, sharing life-giving words, finding where others excel and inspiring them to push past being number seven.

Take action

Fight for what you want

Part of refining who we are as people is pushing through times that don't land in our favor. If you are in a position today and you believe there is more for you, let's dive in a little deeper on how to get there. Just like me in tennis, there were hours of pushing hard not only physically but mentally. I want you to envision whatever you are wanting in your head. Go ahead: play out the vision in your mind. You want to open a boutique? Picture yourself walking into it, the color of the walls, the clothes lined up with your boutique's name printed on the tags. Can you see it? Or how about you are a realtor with dreams of being the top not only in your town, but in the whole state. Picture what it would look like to have your name top that list of great agents. People congratulating you for your hard work and a job well done. When we can envision the success in detail, we can push ourselves to work harder for it.

I did this for myself in tennis: I studied players and would mentally play the scene in my head of me shaking their hand at the end of the match, telling them they fought hard. In fact, the two players I played in the finals of the state tournament -- they were the number one seed -- were the exact people I had in my mind. You may not know who or what you are up against, but playing out that scene and picturing yourself as the winner begins to tell yourself a narrative that is positive and will push you harder than before.

There are two battles that happen when we are wanting to push for something: a physical one and a mental one. Physical would be setting our alarm an hour early to start planning, take that run, eat healthy food, knock on doors, and take action steps. Then there is our mental battle, the one that plays tricks on us. Our minds must be sound in believing that *it can and will be done*. For many people, I was pigeoned into being girl number seven. That was my role, and that was how others saw me. For me, I knew it wasn't true; I knew I belonged on that court.

Often, we let others tell us what they believe to be true about us, when sometimes what they are thinking isn't half as great as what we can imagine for ourselves. You may be on the bottom in your pharmaceutical sales right now, with numbers below the rest of your team. Don't let that define you. Start believing you are the top, the one people are chasing and the one who is hard to beat. When we vision it, we believe it. When we believe it, we will begin to work for it. When we work for it, we become it. Our minds are powerful. The words we tell ourselves become true. Feed your mind greatness, limitlessness, and power. You will only accomplish what you make your mind believe is possible.

CHAPTER 9

Gram

The more people feel seen, the harder they work.

Building a team in your business necessitates encouraging others to perform at their best. When I was fresh out of college and the year before I got married, I packed up my belongings to gamble on myself by opening Tippi Toes in a new state. I drove four hours north to Kansas City and unpacked my suitcases in my mother's childhood home, where I would live with my grandmother. Little did I know that moving in with her for that year, I would gain some of the most valuable business lessons through observing how she lived life.

In her 99 years, she built the most amazing family and community of people who loved and admired her until the day she died. I like to think of this community as Gram's team. She was one of my favorite people I have ever spent time with. My time living with her, I taught dance around Kansas City all day and returned home to her house between 4 and 5 p.m. She would be sitting on her front porch swing, waiting to see what the night had in store for us. Since it was a temporary move for me, I never took the time to make a ton of friends and instead spent time investing in my relationship with Gram. I'd typically visit Adam on the weekends, as he was working on a master's degree two and a half hours away in Wichita, Kansas. My weekdays were filled with teaching dance to children in the city, and my nights were spent hanging out with Gram or other family members. Gram was the very best roommate, always up for doing something fun: she loved to go out to eat, always said yes to ice cream, did all my laundry every single day and had it perfectly folded on my bed when I got home from work, took me golfing, and made sure we caught all of the Kansas City Royals baseball games. When I didn't have early classes to teach, we'd watch the morning talk shows and discuss current entertainment events -- but never anything too serious. We had a difference of opinion on very few things, but she hated the way I ate and told me vegetables and chicken would kill me. She, on the other hand, started her day with a

Vienna Fingers cookie and a short glass of Coke. A complete meal for her was a hamburger, French fries, and a milkshake. She loved people, loved life, loved sports, loved being Catholic, and loved being Irish.

This one-on-one time with her allowed me to learn who she was as a person: her likes, dislikes, values, and goals. I have found the same is important with running my business: the more engaged I am with people on a human level -- vs. employer and employee -- the more tasks we can complete and goals we can reach together. I like to work with people I like. That may sound silly, but it is true. To like people, *truly* like them, you must know them. As we build our business, it is great to brainstorm, problem-solve and complete projects, but equally important to me would be to learn my team's interests outside of work, the books on their to-read list, the restaurants where they've become regulars. Working alongside people you've taken the time to understand as multi-faceted beings gives you context during those moments when work isn't going your way, a project hasn't succeeded as you projected, or a colleague isn't performing up to his or her usual standard. I believe encouraging your own deep empathy makes a person stronger.

Every time we went out to eat or to a ball game or for a walk to the ice cream store, Gram ran into someone she knew. They never failed to stop and talk with her, and she'd proudly introduce me as her roommate. It always floored me how engaged she was in the conversation and how much she retained about the other person. She was a pro. People were attracted to her because she made them feel worthy of remembering. We can do this same thing in business, showing each member of a team that they are of personal value. As leaders, we want to check off the boxes on our tasks and goals when, really, getting to know our staff is the beauty of the project anyway. That collaborative environment fostered by a group of genuinely connected people? Yeah, I'm all about that. There's a major victory to be had in taking a personal interest in, well, *people*. I feel most connected to our Tippi Toes owners not because I know how many dancers they have or what their P&L looks like, but because I know what sports their kids are in, where they are going on family vacation, the important calendar date they have coming up.

One of my last visits with Gram was when I took our kids to visit her for her 99th birthday. She loved them and always said she had the prettiest grandchildren! (The proud mama in me can't say she disagrees.) We walked into her bedroom, the one I had lived in twelve years before, my mother's childhood home. Her drapes and wallpaper were still the same, the double beds sitting side by side facing Morningside Drive, where the sun creeped in to nudge me awake many years ago. I remember lying in that very bed talking to Adam for hours long distance on the phone late at night after Gram and I had eaten our ice cream and said goodnight to one another. This time when I saw her, she began to weep, taken aback that we were actually there. She grabbed me by the face.

"Do you know how much your Gram loves you?" she asked me. Then she put her face in her hands. As she cried, my kids surrounded her with hugs, and she looked up. "I just love having you here and seeing your face," she said to me overtop their heads.

She was completely overjoyed by our short visit. My friend Brooke, a cookie artist, designed cookies that looked like shamrocks, the number 99, and my Gram's house for her birthday. You would have thought by Gram's reaction that we'd bought her a new house. She was overwhelmed by and so thankful for the gift. The amount of time she talked about those cookies and thanked us made *us* feel even that much more special when we were trying to make *her* feel like the special one! Gratitude is another beautiful quality I learned from Gram and have applied to my business, thanking people for simply doing their job. Thanking people for going the extra mile, or for making *me* feel special. When we connect with one another and appreciate the God-given gifts in each of us, the more we all grow.

Have you known someone in your life who makes every occasion notable, like Gram? I'm certain this is where my mom learned to do the same. From the time we were little and my family would drive up from Tulsa to see her, to the times Gram traveled to our house, sent us special cards, or just purely cared for us, her thoughtfulness created a bond. She made little things into big things, in the best way: birthdays were celebrated as weeklong parties, and for the holidays, she pulled out all the stops when decorating her house. She had a large window facing the street, and for each special occasion, she put a big flag up in that window. She was a smile sharer: you would drive by and see her flag and immediately smile. She was a moment-giver and made the most of moments she was given, too. This is how she built her team. She would invest in, pour into, and engage with those who were the most special to her.

Gram thanked me regularly, for seemingly no reason. One time, I pressed her about it.

"Gram, thank you for what?" I asked. "You always say that."

"Thank you for being my friend," she said. "Thank you for being there for me, and thank you for just being you."

I held on to this simple expression of gratitude and try my best to thank people for who they are in my life and for just being them. God made a world of amazing people -- unique, interesting, passionate, and different people. What a gift for us to know and be surrounded by them. Every single time Gram spoke to me, she poured life into me. She knew that to build a strong family, pouring into them was key. Who in your life needs a thank you from you? Has there been anyone who has done something simple yet could use a pat on the back? Kindness and thankfulness go a long way. Who can you encourage today with the simple words "thank you?"

At my last visit to see Gram, she was near death and no longer responding to us. My mom and I stood outside her room in her home in the hallway talking, and she said she'd been praying to God and talking a lot to her mom, knowing Gram could still hear her daughter. I asked my mom what she said to Gram, and my mom's eyes filled with tears.

"I just told her thank you," she said.

My sweet Gram passed away with our family by her side on June 9, 2017. I was holding her hand as she took her very last breath. What a moment of a lifetime. Family filled the room. We knew her time was near, but even at 99, the moment someone leaves this earth still takes your breath away. It was indescribable and beautifully sad all at the same time when I knew she'd passed from this life and we wouldn't talk to her again, but that she would be face-to-face with our Father in heaven. It was wonderful to know the peace she was experiencing, but it also brought us sadness at not having one more story, one more day, or one more smile. We honor Gram still by expressing gratitude.

For the next few days after her death, more family joined in a celebration of her life. To me, Gram was famous because I adored her, but I didn't know if I'd inflated her popularity in my head. The day before her funeral, Adam and I went to her favorite store, Sheehan's -- or as she referred to it, "the Irish store." The woman working there put her hand on my arm as I was checking out and said, "You know, tomorrow you will see what an impact Gram made to all of those in Kansas City." I smiled while surprised she knew I was related to Gram. I told her how special my grandmother had been to me.

"You look just like her," the woman said. Tears rolled down my face. "You may want to walk to her funeral and see the amount of cars lined up to say goodbye. We are all so thankful for your Gram."

I left with a smile, thinking it was really nice for this lady to speak so highly of Gram.

The next day came, and I helped get the programs together for her service. There was a stack of 100 programs. I asked the funeral director if there were any more programs or if he thought this would be enough. He laughed.

"Everybody loves your Gram," he said. "I printed 700."

With Gram being 99, it never would have occurred to me she'd have 700 friends to come to her funeral. In fact, Gram, in her great humor, left "funeral notes" that I believe she wrote in 1980. They read, as only Gram could write, "People to call when I croak." It went on to list eight people, all of whom had died ten to twenty years before her. Needless to say, her notes needed updating. The doors opened to reveal a line of people waiting to get into the funeral service. As the music began and our family walked to our seats, the funeral director pulled me aside.

"We only have 23 left," he said with a huge smile on his face.

That means 677 people showed up to celebrate the life of Gram. I was right about her level of fame: her impact was significant. When my uncle stood at the front of the church, he asked a simple question.

"Please stand up if you think you were Gram's favorite," he said.

You guys, the entire church stood up. Every single person in that church was on his or her feet. Everyone looked around and laughed. My uncle summed up Gram with that one question. She was interested in others. She celebrated others. She sent out hundreds of St. Patrick's Day cards every year. She remembered birthdays, anniversaries, new homes, baptisms, and weddings, and would mail a card on a random day just to make you smile. She became interested in what we were interested in, she loved, she leaned in, and she cared.

These stories of Gram have shaped who I am and what I have tried to instill in Tippi Toes. I was witness to the way she cared for others, and it taught me valuable life lessons. I have taken so many of the moments I lived with her and poured those same expressions into my life and business. I have seen that the more people feel seen, loved, cared for, and thanked, the harder they work and the more invested they become. When someone tries to stir the pot with drama or gossip, give them a hug instead. It may make things awkward at first, but it breaks down walls and allows people into our lives. We must be careful in life, business, at home, or with our friends not to make things about us, but to make things about other people. When we make life about serving others, loving them, and building them up -- like my Gram did -- people see Jesus. Find those who see your vision and want to be part of it, the people who support your dreams even before you do. Then encourage and show up for them in return. Your team will be stronger and better than you could ever imagine when you become others' number one fan. When you take time as a leader to encourage others, it's amazing the type of community you can build around you. I encourage you to show them a little Gram.

Lessons I learned from Gram:

1. **Let people know what you love about them.** As leaders, it is important our employees, co-workers, and customers know we care for them. Knowing the details about their lives helps us

connect on a deeper level, which only serves the relationship.

2. **Celebrate BIG!** Birthdays, anniversaries, start dates at work, promotions, big deals that close, Tuesday, heck, just be intentional about celebrating people in your life and business.

3. **Send handwritten notes often.** I don't know about you, but I love walking down my driveway, opening the mailbox, and finding a letter addressed to me. I love reading thoughtful words in someone else's handwriting. The effort means even more than an email because they paused, found a pen and paper, considered their words, then addressed, stamped, and put it in the mail. Gram wrote thousands of letters in her life to family, neighbors, grocery store workers, mail carriers, restaurants where she enjoyed dining, *The Kansas City Star* for a great story. She told people they were important. She let people know with her encouraging words that what they did and who they were mattered.

4. **Find a passion, and be all in.** (Sports happened to be Gram's!) When we are passionate about

things outside of work, we become interesting and relatable to others. It serves as a jumping-off point for that awkward conversation that sometimes comes with early connection. If nothing else, it gives us something fun to take part in after a long workday!

5. **Don't be afraid to dress up on Halloween as an adult.** Gram had the gift of approachability. Who wouldn't go up and talk to the 96 year old lady in a dog costume? Come on, you instantly adore her. Adding a little Gram to your office will build more camaraderie than you could in a day of back-to-back meetings.

6. **Tattoos: it's okay to get one at 92.** Gram did. Be authentically you. Gram had talked about wanting a tattoo for years. Do you know what stopped her? She was worried what people would think. What she didn't realize is once she got that tattoo, people would love her even more because one, it's an anomaly at her age, and two, we loved her because of who she already was not because of something she did or didn't have.

People are the same way with you; you better believe it.

7. **Remember details about others.** That's what Gram did. She never had a sip of alcohol in her life, but you would never know it because she was the first to walk into a party or a funeral with a bottle of Baileys Irish Cream with a green bow around the neck. She would take a quick trip to Russell Stover and pick up caramels she knew would bring a smile to a friend's face. She remembered what her friends enjoyed and celebrated them the way *they* liked best, not the way she did.

8. **Take walks, and when you do, stop to talk to a stranger.** Never be too busy to meet a new friend or start a conversation. The world has us rushing, and especially in business, we can want to jump from one thing to the next without taking time to stop and truly enjoy all that we are building.

9. **Convertibles make life more fun.** It doesn't have a darn thing to do with business, but it's a true statement.

10. **Love God, and love others well.** Above all else, we are the best leaders when we are connected to God. We love people better, serve them more adeptly, and understand them on a deeper level. Learning servant leadership will allow us to be the best leaders for our companies.

Take action

Show others their value

For Tippi Toes, I feel like our secret sauce is our handwritten notes. Gram told me, "When you take a minute to let someone know you care, they will never forget that." I have learned this to be true in business relationships, and it is one of the things that I think makes Tippi Toes stand out among businesses today. About ten handwritten notes go out weekly from my home office. Often, I'm penning messages to people I've been in contact with that same week. I thank them for the time they took with me, the insight they shared, or the simple detail I learned from them. I love taking a conversation a step farther and making that extended personal connection. Thoughtfulness shouldn't be a rare occasion.

I keep so many of the notes I receive from others, too. It is the perfect cure to pull out of my desk drawer when I need a little pick-me-up, a reminder of what someone believes to be true about me. When I send my notes out, I pray the impact is far longer than the first time they read the note as well. I pray the person reads what I wrote and feels in their bones that they're valuable, important, and special to at least one person in the world: lil' ol' me.

Take a minute to practice this lost art of a handwritten note. List ten people you can write a handwritten note to today, and then *do* it. (Go ahead, I'll wait!)

1.

2.

3.

4.

5.

6.

7.

8.

9.

10.

CHAPTER 10

Build a Great Team

To get others on board, you must believe in yourself

first and foremost.

When I say "Chick-fil-A," what do you think? Most likely the words "my pleasure" come to mind. Cleanliness. Healthy fast food. Friendly service, and the fact that they're closed on Sundays; everyone knows that, because Sundays just happen to be the day we're all craving waffle fries. (Seriously, what gives?) Recently, a group of Tippi Toes owners met Megan and me at Chick-fil-A's Atlanta headquarters to learn about their unique company culture. Chick-fil-A believes in what they call "second mile service," which means going the extra mile, or even more specifically, being servant leaders. As a mom with a full-time job, I constantly battle with creating intentional family time and giving my company the very best of what I have to offer. I believe it's important to spend time with our owners, but visiting all 35 Tippi Toes locations (as of publication time!) would keep me on the road for weeks. I'd been torn between spending quality time with our team and being physically present for my family. With the vulnerability you would expect only from a family member or close friend, while in Atlanta, Megan and I asked a few Tippi Toes owners for ideas. *How do we spend time together as company leaders without taking away from our personal obligations?*

I'm so glad to have had the courage to show my humanity because our team came up with an excellent idea! And they stole it straight off the popular TV show *The Bachelor.* Just like the hometown dates ABC has made so popular on the show, we brought Tippi Toes to my home in Bowling Green, Kentucky. It gave our franchise owners a chance to see me as much more than the polished, motivational coach they chat with on FaceTime. My hope was to connect, brainstorm, and dream, but we did it in the midst of running carpool, keeping up with dirty dishes, battling bedtime, and a ladybug infestation that overtook my house at the same

time as their stay. I opened much more than my home -
- they saw *me*. The real me.

Thanks to Chick-fil-A and our Tippi Toes owners, the
hometown retreat idea was born. But the retreat's actual
structure loosely came from the book *The Five
Dysfunctions of a Team* by Patrick Lencioni. He writes
about creating a space for vulnerability to push the team
forward. In his book, he says off-site group discussion
provides a better understanding of one another. On the
invitation, I specified a strict dress code of yoga pants
and no shoes. In fact, I gifted each Tippi Toes owner with
slippers and a blanket upon their arrival to encourage
informality. What I was able to implement because of
the inspiration from Chick-fil-A was to serve my team
tools on how to build a business: motivation, great
speakers, and planning. But the best thing I learned
during our retreat was that good food, bonding, and
sisterhood are what build culture. And the best part was
being able to do this while at home with my family.

Here are the highlights of our three days together:

Wednesday

- Greeted owners and had my children give them welcome gifts. The power of these gifts went deep because the kids picked them out. Lola carefully wrapped each item in tissue and placed it in a cute pink bag. When she was finished, Hank placed them nicely on the fireplace, where Lucy tagged each bag with a card she designed. Everyone had a job, and everyone felt involved.

- I asked each franchise owner to share her best childhood memory and describe her mentor. We had a room of seven women all sharing their hearts. We heard everything from a sweet memory to the entire life story behind an inspirational adviser. This helped us connect more meaningfully.

- Pam Shaw, the face of Mary Kay cosmetics in our region, spoke about framing each day to get the most out of life. She advised establishing healthy boundaries if we want to make a lasting impact. It was pure validation for me that, as Pam said, "time invested in one area is time away from another." I had made the right choice for my business and my family in this hometown retreat, and I was so proud! There I sat in my own living room, surrounded by Tippi Toes owners with my kids upstairs, within earshot. Oh, how my mama heart just soared and my business mind reeled at the outcome of my creative planning.

Thursday

- We continued talking about our goals and dreams and the adjustments we needed to make to frame our days. Jennie, my sister and a brand-new Tippi Toes owner, shared how she faced the challenge of learning to run a business at 41 years old. She had to deconstruct many of the processes she'd learned over the years working in higher education and rebuild her brain as an entrepreneur.

Rebuilding the Brain

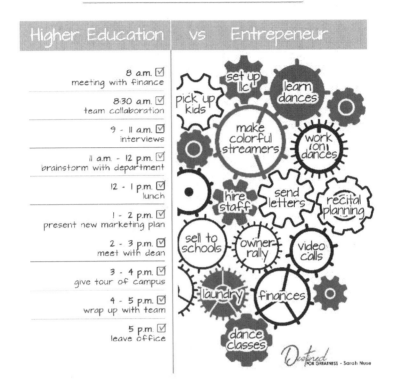

Higher Education | **vs** | **Entrepeneur**

8 a.m.
meeting with finance

8:30 a.m.
team collaboration

9 - 11 a.m.
interviews

11 a.m. - 12 p.m.
brainstorm with department

12 - 1 p.m.
lunch

1 - 2 p.m.
present new marketing plan

2 - 3 p.m.
meet with dean

3 - 4 p.m.
give tour of campus

4 - 5 p.m.
wrap up with team

5 p.m.
leave office

- We talked about our blind spots, the inability to see our own weaknesses. I get it, that's sort of the Webster's definition, but to me, blind spots are not only the inability to see our own weaknesses but the depth it takes to get to our goals. It hurts to acknowledge these weak places in need of work. If you have a good team, your teammates can point out your blind spots. If you have an amazing team, you can talk about those places of opportunity. And that's just what we did. I asked the team, "What will keep you from reaching the goals you have written down?" Some of the responses went like this:

○ I stop believing in myself.

○ I become scared I will fail, and I don't want to hear my husband say, "I told you so."

○ I spend so much time being disorganized.

○ I have a fear of not knowing what to do next.

Now it was time to get a blind spot attack plan.

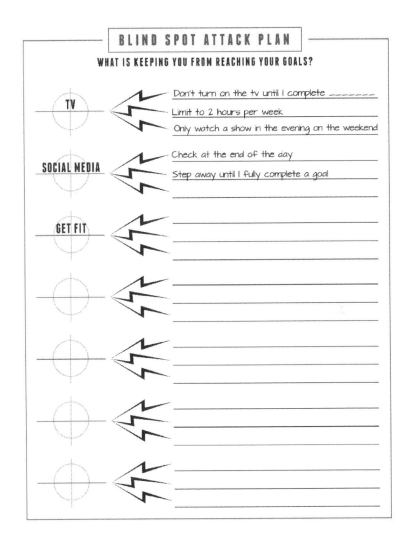

BLIND SPOT ATTACK PLAN

WHAT IS KEEPING YOU FROM REACHING YOUR GOALS?

TV
- Don't turn on the tv until I complete _____
- Limit to 2 hours per week
- Only watch a show in the evening on the weekend

SOCIAL MEDIA
- Check at the end of the day
- Step away until I fully complete a goal

GET FIT

Friday

- Another powerhouse speaker and my dear friend Sarah Frances spoke to us about finding our "why" and living by it daily. (This was a great reminder to me of the time I spent with Bob Goff a few years back. It seems to always come back to the why for me, and perhaps for all of us. I can't stress enough the importance of deeply connecting with your purpose.) She helps lead one of the top pharmaceutical companies as a regional director, managing about 100 people over four states, so, yes, she knows how to lead, empower, and motivate some of the most brilliant people. She encouraged each Tippi Toes owner to have a limitless mindset and live in a place of abundance. A limitless mindset allows us to dream without having to figure it all out first. For example, I could say I want Tippi Toes to be as well known as Coca-Cola, one of the most recognized brands in the world. If I limited my thinking, I would laugh at this major goal, but having a limitless mindset enables me to line up the steps to make it happen. If we can train our mindset to think big, we will always go big, dream big, and, in return, have big things happen. Even if Tippi Toes never reaches the brand awareness of Coca-Cola, I would have stretched myself closer to that point.

LIMITED VS. LIMITLESS MINDSET

GOAL: I want Tippi Toes® to be as well known as Coca Cola®.

LIMITED MINDSET	LIMITLESS MINDSET
Seed of Doubt Planted To be like Coca-Cola, I would have to spend billions, and that's a big investment. Nevermind, I will change my goal.	**Get Momentum Moving** I will come up with a marketing campaign. If that's out of my wheelhouse, I'll hire someone with this skill set.
Downsize My Dream I will instead try to be the business in town that everyone knows and loves.	**Seeking Out Possibilities** I will find all possible avenues to reach the right audience.
Limiting Ourselves I will just try to get ten more dancers.	**Planning for the Next Steps** I will focus on marketing in Bowling Green.
Negative Thinking It seems like all the kids I know are already in dance.	**Taking the Next Step** I will then focus on marketing in Kentucky.
Making Excuses I am actually pretty busy with everything right now. I will get to this later.	**Staying Focused** I will then focus on marketing to the United States.
Moving in Reverse That was such a stupid idea. I'll just stay put. Life is good; what is the point in growing more?	**Moving Forward** I will start a worldwide marketing campaign.
Ending Where We Started To be like Coca-Cola, I would have to spend billions. Nevermind, I will not set a goal. Staying exactly where I started.	**Reaching Our Goals** I will come up with a marketing campaign. Moving the needle to find my audience has grown substantially, and therefore income has increased. Tippi Toes® is nationally recognized.

SUBSTANTIAL GROWTH

This picture is on my refrigerator because it will always remind me of the time I was able to successfully combine business and family. It was a breakthrough moment, and I am still seeing the ripple effect. What I haven't mentioned are the many, many laughs we shared, chips and salsa we devoured, the times I stepped away to help Adam with the kids' baths and bedtime, and the mornings I was still able to drop off my kids at school. Having the audacity to ask for what I needed -- convening with my team without vacating my parental role -- meant I got to have it all. After the friendly insects tried to invade our hometown retreat, the Tippi Toes gang lovingly named themselves "the Ladybugs." Texts between Ladybugs have remained constant since our retreat, encouraging one another, asking questions, and problem-solving. The crazy idea of hosting a retreat at my house with my already hectic lifestyle ended up being the exact bonding experience we all needed. The togetherness leaked into their businesses, creating a powerful connection among this nationwide team and inspiring their franchises to grow. That week, gathered around computers while shoeless and in our yoga pants, we created our own culture, one that could compete with Chick-fil-A any day!

I'm reminded of a time our former business consultant asked if we were trying to build a business or a sorority. The answer he wanted was the opposite of the one I felt in my heart. We trusted him to help us guide our business, but felt sheepish for actually wanting a business that felt like family. Grooming and growing are two different business tactics. He wanted us to groom anyone remotely interested in becoming a Tippi Toes owner while Megan and I wanted to grow our owners themselves -- you know, the whole seed to soil idea. Just like a garden when you are germinating your seeds, we work with women who have the capabilities and passion to run a business but sometimes may not have limitless resources, business knowledge, and -- believe it or not -- in some cases, they lack dance knowledge. Like a seed put in soil, we care for them from conception to growth and long after they're thriving in business. That is what family does. When they become part of our Tippi Toes family, we want them to feel watered, nurtured, given light as they see the sprouts of their business begin to bud.

On the heels of this advice from our consultant, we had a couple request information about our franchise program. From the word go, Megan and I didn't have "that feeling," the one God gives you telling you it's going to work out. With each conversation, there was something off with this husband and wife as potential new owners. They were nice enough, said the right things, but Megan and I were apprehensive. When we voiced our opinion about not wanting to welcome them into our Tippi Toes family, our consultant asked, "How do you expect to make money and grow?" With that condescending response, we shrugged and let them sign the dotted line.

Oh, the dread and trouble that next year as we tried to navigate this unfit match for our company and squish them into the confines of our business! Now instead of truly seeking the right franchise owners to fit our family, our time was spent solely on the wife's wacky and unreasonable requests. It was evident in our business because we went from opening five franchises the year before to just hers that year. We didn't have the time to entertain new candidates because we were constantly hands-on with her. As a franchise owner, she took more than 80% of our time. Ultimately, Megan and I realized we should have gone with our gut, fired the consultant, and got a lawyer to go through the process of removing these owners. So much easier said than done. Another year, where 80% of our time and a lot of money went to moving them out of our business. So, yeah, we couldn't waste one more minute trying to have a business that the consultant recommended; we needed to spend every hour cultivating our culture to draw the "right" people in. Now we can detect early on if a potential owner will fit in like family, and we trust our own judgment. Every single one of our owners has been plucked out of a crowd and grown the Tippi Toes way.

I dreamed of a group of women who fiercely believed in what they were doing, and doing it alongside people they loved. I dreamed of the bonding, the sister-like feel. Tippi Toes gives women the opportunity to be themselves alongside women who are dreaming the same dream. And it's all about impacting the lives of the people around them. So, sure, if my business is sort of like building a sorority, then yes, Tippi Toes is the biggest global business sorority in the history of business sororities. So there.

To me, building a great business isn't enough -- no, not at all. I want roots so deep that this tree will never wither away. I want women to own Tippi Toes and then pass it down to their children and grandchildren. I want Tippi Toes to allow families to maintain a thriving business without their time for togetherness suffering. I want the impact of Tippi Toes to be one that feels like family, from each tiny dancer who joins our class to the teacher who needed a part-time job and every single person in between. To build a great team, and in turn build a great business, you must constantly do both: grow the people in your business *and* allow them to grow their business. So, I guess in my next endeavor, I need to work on the official Tippi Toes handshake.

LIMITLESS MINDSET

GOAL:

Get Momentum Moving

Seeking Out Possibilities

Planning for the Next Steps

Taking the Next Step

Staying Focused

Moving Forward

Reaching Our Goals

SUBSTANTIAL GROWTH

Take action

Specify, find, and encourage the right people

When Adam and I were moving from Corpus Christi, Texas, to Bowling Green, Kentucky, I was excited about the newness. What stared me in the face was how everything in my life at the time was *so good*. Our church, our home team (which was actually our Bible study group), our friends were pointing us to Jesus in a beautiful way. We felt near to God in an unexplainable way. The one fear that crept in had me concerned the move would distract us and it would take a while for us to connect with people in our new community.

This worry led me to write out that which we longed for in our new home. I wanted to be as intentional living in Bowling Green as we were in Corpus Christi. I wanted to surround ourselves with a church family that knew our hearts and challenged our faith in a way that would help us continue to grow. Each desire that bubbled up, I wrote down. I reflected on the qualities I put on this list and knew these were not just ones I wanted in my personal life but in my business life, too. To be surrounded by people who made me and my business better was key for growing spiritually, mentally, and emotionally. I needed to be laser-focused on with whom and where we spent our time. I needed an outline, a checklist to make sure I was being intentional with my life and the people in it. I wanted to design my life so that those around me spoke words of truth and life over me and who I was becoming. I want to do the same to them, too. I am my best when surrounded by those who are also working to live their best.

MY PEOPLE
the people who...

SEE who you are becoming. your dreams & know you can do it. your vision.

SPEAK life.

know what you are **CAPABLE** of.

POINT you to Jesus.

BELIEVE in you.

KNOW your shortcomings but don't highlight them.

PUSH you to be your best.

LIFT you up when you aren't in the room.

when 100 things have gone wrong, **FIND** the one thing that went right.

LET THESE BE YOUR PEOPLE
be this person for others

So, those are the people I'm seeking for my squad. Who do you want by *your* side?

CHAPTER 11

Be GOOD

You don't have to be great; you just have to be good

every day.

Arizona, spring training, and a table of men in a dark, upscale steakhouse. There I sat, not another wife among us at the long, thirty-person table. I had gotten it wrong, or maybe I should say Adam did, or maybe he'd just failed to tell me. Whatever the case, it was me and a table of baseball executives, coaches, and trainers for the Oakland A's -- and my husband. We were there on a work trip for Adam, the trip he told me where many wives joined their husbands as a getaway. Tonight, there wasn't another woman in sight. I was clearly out of place amid the talk about current players and up-and-coming athletes, so I found myself nodding along and playing listener instead of talker. As I eavesdropped on Adam's conversation with Oakland A's manager Ryan Christenson, a light bulb moment happened. Adam had asked him what he looks for when he acquires new players. A simple enough question, but how Ryan responded made a lasting impact on me. He said, "I don't look for the greatest person; I just look for someone who is good every single day."

That's the key in baseball, in business, in parenting, in any area: consistency. I don't have to be the best, but I can be good every single day. Ryan went on to explain that the greatest players come and go, some are high maintenance, some cost too much money, or have too great an ego. He's found that consistently good players equal great success time after time.

A perfect example stared me in the face one day at CrossFit. At my gym, you walk into what I call beautiful chaos. There's a rubber floor where chalk from the previous workout is scattered and chalkboards adorn the wall with workout routines written in a rainbow of colors. You find boxes lined up side by side and towers of weights on rollers throughout the gym, just waiting to be used. The walls are tan with chipping paint, and the building has no heat or air conditioning. Huge fans are turned on only when absolutely needed in the summer. Big garage doors can be thrown open to allow a breeze to sweep through the building. Roaring music blares over the sound of weights being dropped, and sweat is dripped all over as high fives are exchanged. The owners named it CrossFit Old School because they wanted to bring back the "old school" mentality of customer service where the customer is the boss, where first names are used, and where what's happening in each other's lives is really important. This gym isn't anything fancy, but it is an inviting space where fellow athletes become friends and our coaches treat us more like family. This is my gym.

I bring all of this up because something happened while working out one especially hot July day. It was a normal morning for me, exercising alongside the usual crew I've grown to adore over the years. For our workout that day, we ran 600 meters outside with a fourteen-pound medicine ball, then we came inside to do twenty-five double-unders, where you jump rope and the rope goes under you twice instead of just once. The goal of that particular day was to see how many rounds we could do in seventeen minutes. We went outside to our starting spot, the coach counted down three, two, one, and a group of us started to run. I battle it out with my friend Missy at the gym during most workouts. We push each other and encourage each other but, if we are truly honest, we always try to beat each other, too. On this day, there was absolutely nothing I could do to keep up with her -- literally not a thing. It wasn't even like I was in the same league as she was that day. It seemed like she had worked twice as hard as I had and left me in her dust.

This summer, Missy and I had planned to commit to the gym six days a week and stay even longer to lift weights. But guess what? That is really hard to do with three kids on summer holiday, a husband who works an hour away, scheduled family vacations, and a few work trips sprinkled in here and there. My gym commitment went down the tubes fast. In fact, I missed more days than I made it to the gym that summer. I was disappointed in myself but resigned to the fact that the things I chose to do instead of going to the gym held a higher priority for me that summer. You know what was so very evident? The fact that the commitment to work out and get in better shape didn't happen for me, but it did for someone else: Missy not only committed to the summer workout plan of six days at the gym per week and extra weights, but she also got help from a nutritionist whose program allowed her body to fuel properly so she could grow stronger, go faster, and be better. It wasn't like she took a magic pill to beat me so badly that particular day, or, for that matter, many days after that one. My friend and competitor committed and worked hard every single day that summer. While I missed the gym, she put in the time. While I was on vacation, she stayed in the gym for more reps. While I indulged in the feasts that come with summer travel, she calculated the ways to best fuel her body. It was clear: my work that summer was not like hers. It was a physical reminder that if I want to be great, I must be good every single day.

Maybe exercising isn't it for you, but maybe it's your business, your patience in parenting, the side gig you have a strong desire to start, hitting your sales numbers, or kicking a bad habit. When you do the hard work to nudge yourself forward a bit every, single day, you'll look up one day and be the one who beats everyone at the gym, the one with a long-standing business, or the one whose kids impress adults with their kind words and actions. It may be that you blow past all the other salespeople because it was you making those small daily deposits. Maybe it is counting the calories when everyone else isn't, or choosing to say no to a pro bono opportunity when you know it isn't right for you. Whatever it is, you get there by the difficult, everyday work no one sees or applauds you for.

Take action

Consider consistency

Adam is a good representation of small daily deposits in our marriage. He may be oblivious to whether or not wives are invited to a dinner with baseball execs, because to him, we're a team, and he wants me by his side no matter what. He doesn't think twice about signing me up for things he has to attend. Daily, he reminds how he values and appreciates me. He calls out the greatness he sees inside of me, often subtle but always there with a word of encouragement. He can be heard in conversation highlighting things he loves about me, and I laugh because they could be insignificant to whomever he is talking to, but to me, it is *everything*. My parents gave my sisters and me such an incredible example of a mutually supportive partnership, and perhaps without knowingly doing so, I chose a steadfast partner who's capable of holding me up as much as I hold up him.

Marriage, partnership, business, community is a place where we have an opportunity to highlight God with small daily deposits as well. I pray our marriage directs people to Jesus by the way we treat each other. Our dedication to one another isn't for show; it is the real deal behind closed doors, too. The same can be true in business. You might not have a ministry or a church, but you can still call attention to Jesus with your unshakeable spirit. The encouragement we share with our co-workers, commending someone in a meeting in front of the rest of the team, a note on someone's desk reminding them they are doing one heck of a job: this is what builds relationships, marriages, businesses, and community.

To make small daily deposits, we have to be intentional with our time. Every minute matters. So let me help you frame your day with intention:

- What time will you get up in the morning, every morning? Dreams don't rest.

- What will your morning routine look like? Give me the details from getting dressed, to eating breakfast, and everything in between.

- What time in your day will you exercise? Those endorphins that come from working out trigger a positive feeling in the body that's essential to a productive day.

- How much time will you commit to going after your goal? What time of day will you devote to this?

- Who can you list as someone to share your dream with and hold you accountable?

- How will you measure your success (workshop attendance, sales growth, professional partnerships, etc.)?

CHAPTER 12

Cookies with Brooke

Don't try to be Brooke when you are really Sarah.

Celebrating someone else's gifts gives us the ability to recognize how vast and individualized God's gifts are. I believe God gave us specific gifts so we could applaud others, making room for joy, not jealousy. Holding the space of celebration with someone who has fine-tuned their gift reminds us to remain steadfast in our own endeavors. If we can shift our minds from comparing to celebrating, we are one step closer on our journey. It will make us want to keep working, because in my case, making cookies with my friend Brooke was a great example of what a gift looks like when it comes to fruition.

God swiftly reminded me to keep my eyes on my own gifts with a fist to the gut moment one warm summer week. I believed I could borrow someone else's talent, along with the hours of time she had poured into her dream to make the most beautiful cookies you've seen. Have you ever tried to do something that is out of your comfort zone right next to someone who was in his or her complete comfort zone? I did and failed. One of my best friends, Brooke, found a passion and pressed into it. She worked vigorously for years at teaching herself to bake stunningly detailed cookies. I remember our casual conversation so many years ago: "I'm going to be a rock star room mom, and put the other moms to shame," Brooke declared, birthing the idea into the universe. I looked at her like she was crazy because, you guys, neither of us had any kids yet. Her first baby was born a few years after this proclamation, and just like she'd promised, she baked homemade cookies for Connor's third birthday. This particular birthday was a *Toy Story* theme, so she taught herself to make cake pops and cookies in the shape of Woody, Mr. Potato Head, Buzz Lightyear, the aliens, Rex, Slinky Dog, and Hamm. Then she decorated each one of them by hand, distinctive with their own color and design. She worked for weeks, watching videos and researching the best practices on how to perfectly bake and design these sweet treats. She even made practice batches to ensure the big day's treats would turn out wonderful. I remember thinking the amount of time she poured into this party was ridiculous until I walked in and realized, no, this girl has a gift! I looked around at the party in amazement.

"How did you do all of this?" I asked, pushing a bobbing balloon out of my face to get a closer look at Woody's cowboy hat.

"I just taught myself," she said with a smile.

You guys, these cookies she just "whipped up" looked like they could have graced the cover of a baking magazine or won an award for design. They were stunning. Not like the chocolate chip cookies from the Nestlé chocolate chip bag recipe, but sugar cookies cut in unique shapes with impeccable designs. You know the ones you don't want to eat because they're so pretty, but you do want to eat because they taste so good? Brooke was quick to point out the flaws, as we all inexplicably do to downplay our own hard work, but she also kept commenting how easy it actually was to do.

"It looks much harder than it actually is," she insisted.

She kept up this creative art form, making cookies for all our friend group's kids' birthdays, special parties, and events. She followed cookie blogs, read magazines on different design techniques, and constantly tested new recipes. She was all in and thriving!

About six years later, after Adam and I moved away from Texas, Brooke, her husband, and their kids came for a visit in Bowling Green. By this point, she had turned this cute little "homeroom cookies mom thing" into a booming side business. She sold cookies all across the country. I told her I would love to learn how to bake cookies just like her. My mind began to wander away from Sarah's God-given gifts to what it would be like to dabble in Brooke's God-given gifts. As most beginners do, I started thinking I would produce the same quality of cookie she did, although she had six years of experience and plenty of burned, flat, stale, crunchy mistakes on her cookie sheet. *If she could do it, so could I,* I thought to myself.

Well, she lied to me. It was a big, fat lie. I have never labored over cookies so long in my life. There were so many steps! Combining all the ingredients, the waiting, the baking, the cooling, and waiting more, and that didn't even include the decorating. It was a long, exhausting process, and we hadn't even gotten to the fun part yet, in my opinion. As we worked in the kitchen, I started to complain. "I didn't realize this would take us all day," I said. I had plenty of other things I would rather be doing.

"I love it," she said. "It relaxes me." This was clearly her thing.

"No, it is horrible manual labor," I replied.

When the cookies were baked, cooled, and ready to be iced, my excitement returned. Like a child licking dough from the beaters, I couldn't wait for my role in "the easy part." We had 24 car-shaped sugar cookies waiting to be iced for our kids to enjoy. I mixed the colors, put the piping tips in the bags, and followed her directions as closely as I could. We sat side by side while she talked me through every move we were to make. Right about the time she said "and that's it," I was ready to cry. "Easy" was the word I kept hearing, but it was the furthest from the truth for me. When we put our decorated cookies side by side, one may have thought Brooke did the polished, beautiful one and let the kids get ahold of the other. I was a mess, and I failed big time.

You see, because Brooke diligently researched and practiced every single day for several years, much of what she did came naturally by this point. She knew the right spot to hold the icing bag so it wouldn't gush out as fast as mine did. She also knew the specific times to tilt the tip so the icing didn't run. There was one time she put her icing bag in the fridge because it was getting too runny, but I hastily continued. You see, because she had been attentive every day, it came like second nature to her: simple, easy, and even relaxing. She enjoyed studying this art, she enjoyed the challenge, and day by day, year by year, she perfected her art. I, on the other hand, assumed I could pull it off *easily* in a one-day lesson. I quickly realized I didn't have the passion to pursue this cookie art one more second.

When we choose to be good every day, we must make sure it is us following God's plans for our life and not us wishing we could borrow someone else's plans. Jeremiah 29:11 reads, "'For I know the plans I have for you,' says the Lord. 'They are plans for good and not for disaster, to give you a future and a hope.'" We are each created on purpose for God's great plan. Our job is to be earnest in discovering what God's plan is for our life and then use that gift to make a great difference in the kingdom. When we spend calculated time in spaces without our own gifts, we lose the momentum to make a greater impact for God. Being earnest means we take considerable time to listen intently to God, to be still and hear Him. If we chase every opportunity that passes our way, we clog the space for Jesus to enter our minds and our hearts by being sidetracked with all the things of this world. Find your calling and plant yourself in it, discovering how you can impact those around you with the gifts that have been bestowed on you.

I know the only reason I wanted to decorate cookies is because I loved what Brooke did, not because I felt this was a calling in my life, too. We must know the difference between sitting in our sweet spot and desiring a sweet spot of someone else's. I shifted from trying to be like Brooke to supporting her by ordering dozens of cookies and showing them off at some of my life's greatest events! Her cookies have showed up at all my kids' birthdays, at our Tippi Toes *On Top of the World* album release party, and as a gift to Gram on her 99th birthday. I share her work on social media so others can know of her great talent. I decided not to try to copy her and instead highlight her and the hours she devoted in the kitchen. Comparison steals our joy, makes us feel unworthy, and separates us from God. Comparison suffocates our dreams. The opposite is celebration! Celebration allows us to throw confetti on our friends and all their accomplishments, encouraging others to stay in their lane and live life in their sweet spot.

Have you heard that saying "You have the same amount of hours in a day as *you fill in the blank of someone you deem successful* (for me, Jeff Bezos)?" It serves both to celebrate just how much this powerhouse has accomplished and remind us that we, too, are working within the same 24 hours. I had an amazing experience recently at a conference packed with people I've looked up to for a long time, people who I always felt were untouchable superstars in their industries. My plan for the conference was to learn their secrets to packing in as much as possible each day. What actually happened, though, was something so unexpected. I realized these giants in their fields are actually just like you and me. They question themselves, wonder if they are doing the right things, and downplay their dreams. They don't recognize how far they have come but rather see how far they still need to go.

I remember one particular woman, a staple on television for several years, introduced herself to me. She told me her name, and her next words were so powerful that I still think about her honesty. "I'm so nervous," she confessed. I smiled at her and introduced myself while in my brain, I was baffled. Why was she nervous? She was one of the biggest, most well-known stars in the room, and people would be looking to her for advice more than anyone else. As we talked, I asked her how it was being on the television show I knew her from. Her response surprised me. "It was awful. It nearly broke apart my family because of the hours I was working." My face must have clearly shown my shock. I thought, You have one of the coolest jobs in the world, meeting some pivotal people who have done amazing things for our country, and it was awful? I wanted to keep digging, and if you know me well, I have no problem asking 100 questions, so I probed more. Come to find out, she loves plants and nature and has a dream of opening up her own plant nursery. Television wasn't her dream, and while she was there, she didn't feel like she could be who God created her to be. She was on other people's schedules, being told what to say and how to act. From an outsider's view, it looked like she had made it, but she was withering inside.

As I met more and more people at this conference, I realized three things. First, life is not always how it appears on the outside, even for the most successful people. Second, if you are trying to reach your goals and dreams on your own without the guidance of God, it is going to be a lot harder. Lastly, the grass is greener right where your feet lie. We can't waste time sizing up others and wishing our life mirrored theirs. God planted each of us with a distinct purpose. I can't do what you can do, and you can't do what I can do. We are each designed uniquely and authentically. It is wonderful to look up to people and be proud of what they have done, but never allow it to replace all the greatness you have inside of yourself.

Take action

Recognize the gifts in others (and in yourself)

My friend Brooke's gift is so obvious to me and to anyone who witnesses her art. But our own gifts can be less plain to ourselves, leading us to grumble about spent effort without evident outcomes. But I know -- I'm sure of it -- that we each hold a multitude of God-given gifts. Maybe yours isn't cookie art or athletic prowess but instead the ability to make new acquaintances quickly feel part of your friend group or an unending empathy that has co-workers turning to you for advice.

Here's where it gets uncomfortable, friends: if you don't already know your "it," the gift that keeps you up at night and keeps you going during the day, this is where you poll the people in your life. What gift in you do they celebrate? What's the light they see in you that you are blind to?

And then, because this is a place where we recognize each other's talents and honor hard work, list ten people in your life and the good you see in them. What are their gifts? How can you toast to their brilliance?

1.

2.

3.

4.

5.

6.

7.

8.

9.

10.

CHAPTER 13

Keep The Faith

There is no life greater than the one God gave you.

Ever since I met him, my husband Adam wanted to work in sports. He job shadowed baseball executives in high school and set the goal for himself to one day be a general manager of a minor league baseball team. When he got out of college, many of his friends went to work for major corporations, making $50,000 to $75,000. It's a lot of money for young professionals. Around that time, Adam had a mentor who told him it would be wise for him to get a master's degree in sports. While attending Wichita State University, he landed a job with the sports ownership group Ryan Sanders Baseball, working for the Corpus Christi Hooks.

Looking back, working for the Hooks was the best thing for Adam as it laid the foundation for his career, one that started with building culture. One of the first games Adam worked began with picking up trash in the stadium parking lot alongside none other than the big boss himself, Reid Ryan. That night, Adam and Reid were the last to pull out of the stadium. Being in such close proximity to his mentor forced Adam to stay the course. Watching successful people in the business work so hard drove Adam to stay focused. He became a "jock of all trades" in the baseball world. Our Saturday mornings were filled with Adam dressed as the Hooks mascot, bird feathers and all. That's right, Adam ran in the local fun runs on Ocean Drive, a busy roadway in Corpus Christi, as Sammy the Seagull. And when he wasn't, you might have found him in a mullet wig with black scientist goggles over his eyes, wielding a t-shirt cannon in a golf cart as entertainment during the seventh inning. He would do anything and everything. He just kept working hard, determined to be in baseball.

After five years, Adam took a promotion as an account executive with a different team, the University of Memphis Tigers. We were expecting our first baby just four months later, so the move closer to my family in Oklahoma was a no-brainer. It turned out to be a pivotal career move in our life. Working for the Tigers was unlike working for the Ryan Sanders Baseball organization we had loved so much. Adam went from creating culture and thriving in that environment to being stuck in a cubicle making sales calls, a place where he doesn't necessarily thrive. He still focused on being good every day; the seeds that had been planted by being "jock of all trades" and someone who could do it all were what got him to this next point.

It was a Tuesday, and I was six days past my due date with our firstborn. We didn't know what we were expecting, so we lovingly called the baby in my belly "Lanky," a combination of the two names we'd picked out: Lucy for a girl, Hank for a boy. I was humongous. Completely focused on the baby's arrival, I thought nothing of it when Reid Ryan told us he was in town to catch a baseball game at the Memphis Redbirds and wanted to grab breakfast. Afterward, Adam dropped off my family and me while he and Reid went to "check out the Memphis ballpark."

The next night, we headed to the hospital to have our baby. Lucy Ann Nuse was born, making Adam and me the happiest parents in the world. We had all kinds of excitement, and were full of complete joy. A week later, when he couldn't contain himself any longer, Adam told me he would be the next vice president of the Corpus Christi Hooks! Reid's real reason for visiting Memphis was to ask Adam to come back to work in Texas. Adam went on to tell me all the details of his offer, and although it was a move back to the city we had just said goodbye to five months ago, it was an offer we couldn't refuse. Three weeks later, with a newborn, a black lab, and a huge moving truck, we made our way back to Corpus. For me, the move brought a mixture of sadness and excitement. I loved living so close to my family during the few months we'd spent in Memphis, but I also knew what a big opportunity this was for Adam. With the title of vice president, his next move could potentially be attaining his ultimate objective of being a team's general manager. If Adam had drawn a roadmap to that final goal, this opportunity was definitely a stop sign we needed to pass through. Our other two precious bundles, Lola and Hank, were born while in Corpus, making life amazing and busy. Adam loved his job, Tippi Toes was growing across the country, and everything seemed wonderful. We had been settled in Corpus for five years in this position.

It was October, still hot in Corpus Christi with mosquitoes on full prowl. Adam began waking up at night for what seemed to be no apparent reason. He was restless and couldn't sleep, which became his new normal for about eight weeks. Work was great, he loved his family, and we were surrounded by an amazing church and some of the greatest friends. Adam couldn't put his finger on it, but like clockwork, he was awake every single morning at 3 a.m. I'd see the glare of his phone screen, as he would be up reading or playing games to try to settle his mind. One morning, while we both brushed our teeth, Adam said a sentence I will never forget.

"I sent an inquiry last night to buy a minor league baseball team," he said with a wad of toothpaste in his mouth and some dripping off his lip. I just looked at him, puzzled. "The ad said 'Red hot deal in the Midwest,' so I figured I would go for it."

I smiled because Adam thinks big, and all I could respond with was encouragement. "Great!" I said. "I hope that works out." Then I shrugged it off so quickly because, you guys, the raise he got from moving from Memphis to Corpus in no way put us in any range to buy a baseball team. It was honestly comical, but I know Adam, and I don't put much past him. Baseball team, it is!

A few weeks later, Adam called me on his way home from work. "Remember when I tried to buy that baseball team?" he asked. "Well, someone beat me to it, but they called because they need a general manager."

My first thought was, *Let's go!* I love moving to new cities, meeting new people, becoming familiar with a new environment, new grocery store, new stomping grounds. I feel closest to God when I am stretched outside my comfort zone, solely relying on Him to comfort me and guide me through all the newness. This was exhilarating for me, and I was up for the challenge. Tippi Toes was going great in all aspects, and our kids were the perfect ages for an adventure, so I didn't hesitate. At this point, we still didn't know what city this team would be in because the ad Adam responded to just spoke of a team in the midwest. When I looked up midwest it listed ten different states that encompass that area. Over the next few weeks, Adam talked to the owner for the team and found out this team was in Bowling Green, Kentucky. The town was much smaller than Corpus, with a quaint little downtown with black wooden fences holding back horses. It was sweet, and immediately felt like home. We stopped to see the ballpark and meet the owners. It all seemed in line with what we were looking for at the time. With a firm handshake and a press conference at the age of 32, Adam made another huge jump in his career to that of a general manager running a single A baseball team. Goal accomplished!

Those restless nights and lower-paying jobs weren't without purpose; they were part of his path leading here. Lots of hours at the ballpark, tarp pulls, sales meetings, foul balls, seventh inning stretches, and fireworks shows had gotten him to this point. After working nearly 1,000 baseball games, he was now the man in charge. He leads by example by being side by side with his staff: he'll take out the trash, clean up the suite, set up for an event, make the cold call, deliver tickets, walk around the office handing out high fives and sometimes Natty Lights, reload the toilet paper --

okay, no he doesn't, I took it too far -- but the list goes on.

Proverbs 20:24 says, "The Lord directs our steps," and this was such tangible evidence that God was doing just that in our lives. Adam may have lost sleep, but he gained tenacity. Our story is best when we allow God to walk in and start steering us to where he wants us to go. I am thankful Adam chose to keep his eyes focused on where God planted him. He was intentional with the desire the Lord put on his heart. The beautiful thing about dreams is they continue to grow and change, just as we do. When I thought we were settled in as a family forever in Bowling Green, Adam made a realization.

"I can't reach my dream at 32," he told me one day. "I need to find a new dream."

I loved this sentence from him, but I corrected him. "You can reach your dream at 32, but now you just need to reach for a new one."

Dreams and goals *should* be ever-changing because the hope is to reach them and then keep stretching beyond them. Just because 32-year-old Adam reached the goal he had set at 18 didn't mean he was finished. It meant God was going to allow him to be creative and aim for something new to stretch him and grow him.

While living in Bowling Green, we were fortunate to be near Western Kentucky University. Adam knew if he wanted to dream bigger in the sports industry, continuing his education could push him forward faster. He kept feeling that nudge from God, so he applied and got accepted to WKU's doctoral program. While working toward his doctorate and after his third year with the Bowling Green Hot Rods, he got a call from the owners of the Nashville Sounds. Nashville has a triple A team in the heart of downtown, with a brand-new baseball stadium. He didn't anticipate they wanted to meet about a job opportunity, but he was wrong: they had their eye on Adam and wanted him to run the team in Nashville. Not only was it a jump in leagues, but also the entire operation was bigger than what he had run in the past. For our family and for Adam's career, this was a big deal.

Today, Adam -- or should I say Dr. Nuse? -- is the general manager of the Nashville Sounds. He finished his doctoral program and continues to dream big, is innovative in bringing new ideas to the ballpark, and is passionate about impacting the lives of those around him. To me, he's an absolute all-star.

As I've established, my dream has always been to share Jesus with everyone I meet. In 2018, I had been specifically praying to God to use me in a big way to bring light to others. I used to struggle with the fact that I might need to be in ministry to get this accomplished, but allowing God to lead, he creatively positioned me into a life-changing moment. I was having lunch with my friend Brandi Wilson, who was telling me about a trip she took to Thailand visiting the slums of Bangkok. The purpose of the trip was to see the great need in Thailand and figure out a way to be of value. Sex trafficking is at an extremely high rate, and young girls are forced into this lifestyle because they have no choice; their only way to make money is selling themselves to feed their family. Brandi's story overwhelmed me. She shared about a preschool she visited that cared for and educated the area's children, all of whom had mothers trapped in slavery.

As Brandi talked, I became overwhelmed thinking of the broken cycle and the need for hope, dreams, and laughter for these small children. She suggested there might be a way to use Tippi Toes to bring them happiness and some semblance of normalcy, if only for the duration of a class. I responded with "Oh, I would *love* that." She connected me with Noel Yeatts, the president of World Help, a Christian humanitarian organization. Together with Noel, Brandi, and a few other women, I boarded a plane and flew halfway around the world to Bangkok, Thailand. This was out of my comfort zone. I had never been this far from home, and I was with a group of women I had just met. I had to say yes if I was going to live out my why. I felt God calling, and I wanted -- needed -- to answer.

When we arrived, we visited many of the women who were trapped in slavery, as World Help partners with amazing organizations to help free these women. Night after night, meeting with girl after girl, I was left feeling empty and vulnerable. I had trouble sleeping as the images of what I witnessed were etched in my mind. Evil. The devil. Darkness. Hopelessness. I kept asking God, "What can I do? Why am I here?" On the third day, Noel notified us we would be going to the slum to bring food to the elderly and visit the preschool. She asked if

I would be willing to dance with them. I was unsure what this would look like but willing to do whatever I could to help.

We walked into the school to see fifteen quiet, well-behaved children sitting around a table listening to the teacher. My eyes welled up with tears as I thought about the lives they have, so different than any I have seen in the United States, so different from my own children's situation. For homes, they had plywood stuck on a mud floor with a tin roof over head -- if they were lucky. There was no heating, no air conditioning, and little to no food. The slums smelled like rotten sewage. I sat with these children, colored, tried my best to communicate through a warm smile.

Noel turned to me. "Are you ready to dance?" I smiled and got my music ready, but if I am honest, I wasn't sure how this would go. The children were very shy, and there was a sense of them being unsure about all of us there. They gathered in a circle on an outdoor covered pad of concrete -- it had to have been at least one hundred degrees -- and looked at me with blank stares. I turned on the very first song we wrote for Tippi Toes, called "I love Tippi Toes." I began to dance, and just like that, they all started following along. Their blank stares turned to giggles as we jumped, leaped, and sang. I brought out colorful streamers for them to use for our next song. The beauty was deep within their smiles. The next song I turned on was one I had written six months before, called "Learn from One Another." As the music played, I began to tear up, yet again. Only God. God does this. He knew I would be in this position dancing with these kids halfway around the world, but I didn't. He laid the path yet again. It was at this moment I realized I *was* in ministry. Not the type where I run a church, but the kind where I run a company that not only brings joy to children in the United States but can impact children around the world.

My "why" became crystal clear. God groomed me for this moment: all the dancing, the ideas, and dreams, I believe, were to get me to this point. It is a moment engraved in my mind forever, the moment heaven met earth. I began to see how we all have a purpose. Tippi Toes touched U.S. communities in a large way, but now we have the capability to reach those who, due to their circumstances, may never get the chance to live out their dream. Tippi Toes's mission became more than instilling a love of dance in children: we decided to partner with World Help in letting others know about the opportunities they have to sponsor children on the other side of the globe. Seeing those sweet faces in the preschool allowed me to see the greater need. Knowing Tippi Toes can make a difference through our voice and connecting others with World Help, how they are changing the world, lets us be a small part of what they are doing.

It wasn't about dance this day. It became more, and for many, many days after. All of our franchise owners came on board, many sponsoring children and sharing this idea with their customers. Tippi Toes now has families saying yes to children they never met.

Take action

Position your purpose

You were made with great purpose. We all have those secret thoughts and wishes for our life. Sometimes they are so grand and big we don't even want to say them out loud. Come in close for a second -- a little closer -- and let me whisper something to you: *God designed you for that right there.* He placed those very wishes inside of you. Why not dream big? What can you do to set yourself up for the best possibility of living out your life's purpose? For my husband Adam, that looked like saying yes to opportunities that meant we'd need to create a new home in a new place, which is both exciting and scary for anyone. For me, it meant saying yes to an opportunity to travel to another country and witness heartache in order to construct a meaningful giving-back initiative for Tippi Toes. It's one of our proudest ventures to date.

I'm realizing now, as I write these very words, that positioning your life to live out God's design so often means saying yes even when you can't foresee the outcome. Could Adam have predicted that dressing as Sammy the Seagull would one day lead to him serving as the general manager and COO of the Nashville Sounds? Heck, no. Did I know I'd be able to communicate with these Thai children through our shared language of dance? Okay, maybe I had an inkling, because I've long known the connective power of movement, but I couldn't have foreseen our long collaboration with World Help.

My counsel to you is this: say yes. Take the meeting, join the organization, plan the trip -- whatever it looks like. Agree to see where the opportunity might lead, and by all means, arrive there with an open mind and a willing heart.

CHAPTER 14

What Seeds Are You Sowing?

Soil responds to seeds, not wishes.

She has goals, real goals. She wants to be a trailblazer in our company. She wants to impact the life of 500+ dancers in her city. She wants to make a monthly income that many consider a yearly salary. My ambitious colleague outlined each specific goal on paper, and I was going to help her get there. Her time is hers -- not a husband, a child, or even an animal to tend to. What could possibly get in her way?

Soil responds to seeds, not wishes. In the Bible, Jesus shares a parable of the farmer scattering seeds. In Matthew 13:8: "Still other seeds fell on fertile soil, and they produced crop that was thirty, sixty, and even a hundred times as much as had been planted!" When we sow our seeds (our dreams and goals) in fertile soil (daily action steps, right conversation, hard work, diligence), we reap much more than our input.

I host a virtual accountability group that focuses on drilling in habits to get each business owner to her specific goals. The impetus for its creation was to help my franchise owners remain focused while trudging along toward their goals, and it's grown so much bigger than I expected. The same goes for the individual's experience: we see tremendous growth during the month we spend together. Participants receive a group message from me in the morning and evening each week day to set the focus. I find it helpful to tackle problems in small pieces instead of expecting ourselves to master everything at once; for example, I'll ask group members to be mindful of specific activities for a day, like distractions, uninterrupted time, sleep schedule, etc. (It seems much easier this way than to tell yourself, "I won't look at social media, and I'll set aside four straight hours of work time, and I'm going to get nine hours of sleep every, single night!" You just set yourself up for failure that way, don't you think?)

Due to the success of this group, I've opened the accountability up to other dreamers. I have found the same thing to be true: when we are focused, make daily deposits, and are held accountable, we see life change. Today, I host about six groups a year, each lasting one month. The progress and growth for these participants has been beautiful. (For opportunities like this and others, go to www.sarahnuse.com.) The group's first task is to fill out an hour-by-hour schedule to see where the owner plans to spend her time. My colleague turned in her accountability log for day one of my program. It looked like this:

5 a.m.	Sleep
6 a.m.	Sleep
7 a.m.	Sleep
8 a.m.	Wake/dress/eat
9 a.m.	Teach TT class
10 a.m.	Grocery store
11 a.m.	Return phone calls
12 p.m.	Meet a friend for lunch

1 p.m.	Friend/check email
2 p.m.	Team conference call
3 p.m.	Teach TT class
4 p.m.	Teach TT class
5 p.m.	Friends for happy hour
6 p.m.	Happy hour
7 p.m.	*Bachelor* season premiere
8 p.m.	*Bachelor* season premiere
9 p.m.	*Bachelor* season premiere
10 p.m.	Relax

Can you see which activities are getting in the way of her reaching these goals?

When she sent me this schedule, after I picked myself up from the floor in disbelief, I went through and highlighted the activities that I saw were bringing her closer to her goal. There was only one: her 2 p.m. team conference call. The rest of the activities were either keeping her right where she was or even lessening the chances of making her dreams happen. Her actions didn't match her goals. Something needed to change -- either her goals or her schedule -- so we had a conversation and fine-tuned her schedule:

5 a.m.	Sleep
6 a.m.	Wake/dress/eat
7 a.m.	Quiet time/Reading
8 a.m.	Sales
9 a.m.	Teach TT class
10 a.m.	Sales/podcast
11 a.m.	Sales/return phone calls
12 p.m.	Friend for lunch/emails
1 p.m.	Sales/podcast
2 p.m.	Team conference call

3 p.m.	Teach/with potential hire
4 p.m.	Teach/with potential hire
5 p.m.	Interview new employees
6 p.m.	Marketing plan
7 p.m.	Happy hour/dinner
8 p.m.	Write a plan for tomorrow
9 p.m.	*Bachelor*/ready for bed
10 p.m.	Bed

By making these shifts, she could take action steps toward her dreams, creating ten hours in her schedule to do productive work. In his book *Atomic Habits,* James Clear writes, "One of our greatest challenges in changing our habits is maintaining awareness of what we are actually doing. This helps explain why the consequences of bad habits can sneak up on us." Frequently, it's fine-tuning what we are doing and making ourselves aware of our daily choices that allows us to make the changes needed to move forward. With that in mind, we looked at her schedule and made these simple changes:

- Waking up and starting her day two hours earlier

- An hour of quiet time and reading as deposits toward her personal growth

- Building in time to grow as a salesperson

- Listening to a podcast while driving to sales calls to constantly pour information into herself -- a little trick I refer to as "habit heaping," stacking good habit upon good habit, throughout the day.

- Teaching *with* a potential hire to see if potential candidates are qualified for the job

- Intentionally planning for the next day

Matthew 3:10 reads, "Yes, every tree that does not produce good fruit will be chopped down and thrown into the fire." This verse struck me as I was studying the Bible about living a fruitful life because it's so easily applied to our schedules. If we want to reach our goals and dreams -- the "fruit" -- we must be willing to cut out those activities that do not allow fruit to grow. What in our schedule is not producing fruit in our life? The extra hour spent watching TV, an inconsistent bedtime, games on our phones, being unorganized and misplacing needed items? What we did in this exercise was first assess what was really happening in her day versus what it *felt* like was happening in her day. I find we think we work more than we actually do because of the time we spend thinking about what we should be doing. (You follow?) Our time is so important, as is how we value it, and what we do with it can change our life.

So how do we trim the dead branches in our schedule? We must first see what our schedule looks like by writing it down. After it is written, follow it. In my accountability group, we use check marks and x's to see how well we are tracking. We track from 6 a.m. to 10 p.m., every day. If a person follows what she said she was going to do in the hour, she gets a check mark. If not, an x. Each day, the group reports back to me how they tracked. The goal is 17 check marks. What happens over time is we see tendencies and habits that interrupt living an intentional life.

One of our participants complained of being so tired all the time. After looking at her schedule, she put "bedtime" at 10 p.m. each night. What we saw was she never made it to bed on time, resulting in an x each time. What was happening is she was telling herself she was going to bed at 10 p.m. but really, actually falling asleep at midnight. Her workday started with her alarm chirping at 5 a.m., giving her only five hours asleep. She always felt behind, running and scrambling, full of exhaustion. Mentally, she thought she was going to bed at 10 p.m., because that was when she went into her bedroom. However, she brought her laptop with her to work for another hour in bed, and claimed then she needed "time to unwind," so she vegged out in front of the TV for another hour. This was wasted time and stole time from her the following day. It took the accountability of having someone else examine her schedule to open her eyes to this. That is what being held accountable does: it allows us to see areas where we are on autopilot and therefore not able to move forward and experience growth.

Could you be convincing yourself of a schedule that isn't your reality? Try it. Join me! Sign up for accountability at www.sarahnuse.com, and start living your life full of intention and purpose.

Take action

Detail your days

2 Timothy 1:7 reads, "For the Spirit God gave us does not make us timid, but gives us power, love and self-discipline." Self-discipline doesn't mean being hard on ourselves. It actually has us making things *easier* for ourselves through removing distractions from our daily life and becoming fully engaged and active toward our dreams.

- How many hours do you believe you are working toward your goal each week?

- Spend the next week filling out an hourly log to see the hours spent toward your goal.

- What's in your schedule now that doesn't *have* to be? What can you hand off to someone else or remove from your life because it doesn't serve you?

There is a blessing waiting for each of us. It's time for you to take action today on those ideas inside your heart. I challenge you to get so busy loving God, loving others, and chasing that dream inside of you that you don't have time for worry, regret, or fear to sneak into your schedule; the only option is taking action. Start where you are, with what you have, and move forward. Look at your days and get rid of the dead branches to start producing a life of fruitful limbs. Great accomplishments never come from comfort zones. Get comfortable with being uncomfortable, and press into your dreams. Your life is too valuable for you to not be fully engaged.

- What is it that you need to take action on right now, most immediately?

- What can you do right now to move your idea forward?

- Who can you share your idea with, either as a means of being accountable or to make a possibly fruitful connection?

CHAPTER 15

Loss of Focus

Panties on your head

My sister Jennie knew I needed to relax. The hiss in my voice over the phone gave it away. "No!" I yelled, partially into the phone, piercing Jennie's ear as my kids spilled a drink on the pile of freshly folded laundry. It was Kool-Aid. Red, at that. It wasn't my normal go-to, but I was out of tricks and at that moment. I was *done*. With three kids under age three at home and a booming business that seemed to need my constant attention, my defeat was evident. Jennie soon gifted me with a one-hour massage to untangle my mind from schedules and routines, and press out every knot in my shoulders.

I arrived 30 minutes early so I could sit and relax in peace. There was a strong release from my shoulders as

I walked across the fragrant garden -- did I detect lavender and eucalyptus? -- through the large wooden doors, and into the spa. Peaceful wind chimes danced together while I checked in with the front desk. Soothing spa music played, and I let myself sink into an indulgent placid, calm. They handed me a key and showed me to the ladies locker room, pointing out my fluffy white robe, slippers, shower cap, shower essentials, and disposable panties. Tying a knot in my robe, I filled up on fresh cucumber water and headed to the quiet room. I turned the corner to see a lady sitting on a black, cushioned chaise lounge chair with her eyes closed, enjoying her quiet time. I couldn't help but notice she had gotten it all wrong, and I mean *all wrong*. There she was, sitting in serenity, with the disposable panties placed perfectly on her head. She had mistaken the shower cap that was in her locker for the disposable panties and had the panties perched on her head like they were supposed to be there. As she practiced her deep breathing, I tried to catch my own breath from laughing so hard. How could she get it so wrong? As my giggles faded and I lay beside her waiting for my name to be called, I began to think about the many times I, too, had gotten it all wrong. There was that time my sweet kids didn't know I was under a deadline for work, was running on too little sleep, and snapped at them for asking one too many questions. Hence, my making this time for myself at the spa to reset my patience.

Could you be walking around with panties on your head, getting it totally wrong because you aren't paying close enough attention? Distraction comes in different forms. Remember the Bible story in which Martha extended the invitation to Jesus to come to her home? While he was there, her sister Mary sat at Jesus's feet listening to every word he said. Luke 10:40 reads, "but Martha was distracted by the big dinner she was preparing." She even got frustrated at her sister and complained to Jesus. She was so focused on the big meal and not Jesus being in her presence. The exact same can be true for us.

I remember one of the most humbling moments in my life when I got distracted. I was in high school and playing on my school's tennis team, which I barely made (see Chapter 8). At that same time, I also had the desire to be on the dance team. *How hard could it be to learn a dance and perform it to make the team? I am a dancer, after all* -- or so I thought. Well, it was time for me to take a bite of humble pie, because I totally failed.

On the day of the dance team audition, I felt butterflies in my stomach when the MC called my number over the loudspeaker. I knew I wasn't as prepared as I should be because I had missed every rehearsal that week, excused so my tennis team would have enough players. I was told I could practice by myself at home, which never happened. Somehow, I still was confident it would all just come to me in the moment. The gym was filled with lots of girls hopeful to make the dance team. About 200 parents, siblings, and friends were there to cheer us on. As I stood in the middle of the basketball court to get ready to dance, I put my head down in the starting position. Standing just behind me were a few upperclassmen from the dance team who would do the routine along with me so the judges could see if I was doing the correct steps.

The music came on, and at first I froze. *"Did they put on the right song?"* I remember thinking. Then I just started to dance -- though not the dance we were supposed to do or one anyone had ever seen before. I guess somewhere in my mind, I thought I would just dance any dance, and maybe they would like it, even if it wasn't remotely correct.

It was an out-of-body experience. I knew the dance routine just enough, but I hadn't spent the week drilling it in my head step by step like the other girls. I was unprepared because of my focus on tennis. The time I spent learning the dance was what little time I had leftover after tennis, homework, and hanging out with friends . (This *was* high school, after all.) I didn't make the dance team audition a high enough priority, so I failed. In the middle of my original routine, a loud voice boomed over the speaker as the music came to a sudden stop. The coordinator made an announcement in front of all 200 people in the gym: "If you can't come prepared to perform, you are wasting our time. Please exit the floor." I was the very first to get stopped in the middle of the routine. This hadn't happened in any other dancer's audition.

She was right. I was ill-prepared, but it still hurt so badly to be instructed to leave in front of my classmates and their supporters. I was trying to juggle too much and therefore failing, and in front of a lot of people. I was not laser-focused on the dance; rather, I was doing the bare minimum, hoping I could skate by and still make the team.

It's funny now to think I run a dance company spanning across the United States and into other countries, even after getting humiliated trying out and completely being rejected from my high school dance team. I could have let that distract me and completely block my view from what God intended for my future. I could have let this failure define me and tell me I wasn't good enough. The truth of it was I knew I hadn't prepared for the audition. I knew I had more in me, if I had just given more attention to my preparation. My eyes were focused elsewhere, and there was a reason other dancers made the team while I didn't. I never would tell anyone that I'm the greatest dancer, but I love it and I love what Tippi Toes does for kids around the world. I love that we get to build children up, take them on magical adventures, and speak life into them through our dance program. I let this lesson about what happens when I'm distracted push me into more of my purpose.

The same could be true for you. You might not be the best, but maybe you love your craft the most. Lean into it, and don't let your attention be diverted. God gives us those desires in our heart, and if we passionately follow and sow the seeds, we will reap a harvest. One thing that blows my mind when I recount this story is how my family acts like they can't remember it happening. To me, it was a moment time stood still; to them, it was just a Thursday. I remember empathetic hugs from my family and encouraging words, but it wasn't a defining moment to them. While we're the stars of our own movies, we're the supporting actors in the movies of others. Our humiliation is our own, and witnesses to it will soon forget it. I think this perspective is important to remember.

Take action

Recast your defeats

The times I have fallen flat on my face are the moments that have grown and matured me the deepest. I hate the feeling of embarrassment, loss, or defeat -- raise your hand and explain yourself if you look forward to that feeling! -- but every single time, I have taken away a great lesson. Adam tells me he hates when I claim these as "failures" because he thinks they truly are just growing pains while we mature as people and leaders. Could it be the same for you? When you have been faced with disappointment or growing pain in your life, how have you pushed past the pain to see it benefit your entire life? My list of growing pains continues to grow. I have learned that instead of feeling defeated and frustrated with my shortcomings, I look at them to figure out how I can use this frustration to launch me into something even greater. You can do it, too, as with every failure you are one step closer to great success.

Often, we highlight our failures and flaws by assigning them more value than they merit. When really, if we dig deeper into them, we find that these have been our greatest teaching moments. What are some so-called "failures" you've been stuck thinking of as setbacks that really have led you on to something so much greater? Think back to some growing pains. Now reflect on how you grew. (Remember: pain equals growth.)

CHAPTER 16

It's Not Always What You See.

I put on a pretty smile, but I wanted to leave.

Comparison can take the wind right out of your sails. This feeling easily arrives from the lies we tell ourselves and what *appears* to be true rather than what is reality. It can be so frustrating to feel like you're making headway toward your goal only to open social media and find someone else two miles ahead of you. It can be equally frustrating to see a private dream you thought of as yours and yours alone to have already been brought to life by someone else.

Deception and the stories we tell ourselves can stunt our growth as business leaders and keep us from the very place God has called us to be. A perfect example of this is when I think about a trip Adam and I took to Hawaii. From social media, it appeared as though we were whisked off on a work trip for Adam while our kids were home with my parents. Everything was happy and perfect. Why would people think this? We posted a picture of us at the airport getting ready to take off, we posted a picture of the beautiful blue-green water from our balcony when we arrived, and we posted a picture with Adam's arm around me while we both wore leis at a Hawaiian luau party.

What we didn't share were the numerous calls I made to the doctor to try to get medicine because I felt so terrible. We didn't share the picture of me taking Tamiflu, cough drops, Mucinex, and Nyquil and the countless boxes of tissues I used in the first 24 hours of arriving, or the tears streaming down my face on our flight because the pressure in my ears was unbearable. We also didn't post me sprawled out in our hotel room with a pillow on my head while the blue skies were sunny, the surfers were hanging ten, and the waves crashed against the shore. Nor did we post the face I gave Adam when he asked me within eight hours of landing, and me feeling horrible, if I wanted to shark dive. *Shark dive*, of all things, while my head felt as big as a house. Why didn't we post all of that? It's just not all that glamorous. Certainly not part of the highlight reel. It was a very, very low part. To be honest, the last place I wanted to be was in some random hotel room in Hawaii away from everything that is comfortable to me, including my doctor, my bed, and my bathroom.

Social media portrays the absolute peak in a person's day, week, or month. It is polished, filtered -- and anything but reality. Sure, we might've been in Hawaii and having fun, but these pictures didn't share the entire story. When we view posts like this, some of us may end up creating a storyline about what we believe another's life to be like based off a carefully curated snapshot we see on their social media account.

So often we try to juggle this life to make it appear perfect. The truth is that it is *really hard* to juggle it all and make it perfect. In fact, no one can truly achieve this effortlessly. If you are a stay-at-home mom, you don't feel you have anyone who gets it. You are with your amazing children all day, but that's just it: you are with them *all day long*. That means lots of time for snuggles, which is awesome, but that also means lots of homemade meals, which then equal lots of cleaning up, pouring milks, wiping counters, and sweeping floors, only to repeat the monotony for the next meal. Not to mention navigating meltdowns when refusing to allow a child to just wear her undies to the store because she is too hot to put on clothes or handing over *the absolute wrong t-shirt* to wear for the day. (Anyone else have a toddler at home?) We are changing diapers, wiping noses, singing a cartoon song that's stuck in our head, and swapping out laundry, and our sole social interaction with people of voting age is the occasional Facebook scroll to see what other adults are doing, or a play date that takes two hours of preparation. We don't (often) complain because we love and value it, but day in and day out, it does get exhausting.

If you are a work-from-home mom like I am, the hats you wear just keep piling up. Your morning email scan reminds you of the millions of tasks calling your name, then you wake kids, make breakfast while taking a work call, do laundry while responding to an email, mute a conference call to solve a child's problem. You are pulled in multiple directions from the time you wake to the time you sleep. You master the mom duties as best as you can, try to make your work look presentable, and are dog-tired by the end of the day.

Then there are the full-time working women. You kiss your babies goodbye at daycare to work your tail off while away from them. While you are at work, you feel like you should be with your baby, but if you are home, you feel like you need to be working. Your laundry still piles high at night when everyone sheds their clothes, dinner still must be planned and executed, and often, since you feel like you haven't seen your kids much during the day, you let bedtime linger and sometimes fall asleep next to your little one just to get a few more minutes with them. But, friend, you are worn out, too. You struggle, and you juggle. I see you.

If you saw what my years as a work-from-home mom looked like, I'm sure a lot of you could relate. Those years included a severe lack of sleep at all times, three toddlers at home, the cupboards bare from not having a moment to myself to venture out to the store, a messy house, diaper changes, potty training, toys everywhere, dishes stacked to the brim of the sink, a serious backlog of emails, a full voicemail, a husband who worked around the clock providing for all of us, and a lonely mom trying to make it all work. It was so hard. We have never been fortunate to live close to family, so this period of our life was Adam and me just trying to survive.

About this same time, that amazing little time-waster Pinterest came about. At night while rocking a newborn Hank to sleep, I'd scroll through endless possibilities. At first, I fell in love with it, thinking of all the ways I could change the kitchen or revamp the laundry room, or redecorate the kids' playroom into a magical land. When I saw the pictures of final reveals posted and the quick one, two, three steps, I believed I, too, could replicate the same looks. Quickly, though, I felt this app reminded me how my house was out of date, my parties were less than perfect, I didn't have enough time, and my wardrobe needed to be completely redone. Instead of Pinterest being a fantastic tool for me, I looked at it and only saw all the things I didn't do well.

What a terrible way to think, right? Honestly, this was my state of mind. I was in a funk, needed sleep, and had a lot of babies needing my attention. Reflecting on this time, I know now that all the emotions I felt were just a product of motherhood's trials. It's all-consuming. You love so much it hurts, you care so much you cry, and you try so hard that you just want to curl up into a ball and sleep for hours and hours (and hours). My work on Tippi Toes began to slip because I was so focused on my three little ones being at home with me.

Our Corpus Christi pastor's wife, Jessica, called while I was in this season of life to ask if I would be interested in filming something for Mother's Day. She had grand visions of showcasinging my home in its normal state of disaster. It would be shown at all of our church services to relate to mothers as part reality and also a little comic relief. I, of course, said yes because that's what we do as women. If you are like me, you say yes when it needs to be a no because we are wired to be pleasers. Jessica's request was for the camera crew to come to our house and film life as it actually was. She told me to not clean up because they wanted real life, and she said not to do any dishes because she wanted to use those as part of the shot. She wanted the video to be completely relatable. It sounded easy enough -- until the day actually came around.

My house was, as it normally was in this life stage, a big ol' hot mess. Toys blanketed the living room, piled the stairs, and spilled into the kitchen. There was clean laundry (oh yes, did you catch that, friend? It was actually clean!) stacked high with tons of outfits discarded around the house from the kids playing dress up. Last night's dinner dishes were still out because I was too tired to clean them the previous evening, and this morning's breakfast dishes were scattered on every counter. Hank ate waffles in his high chair that morning and tossed one over the tray right where our black lab, Wrigley, decided to roll, so there was a pile of syrup caked with dog hair stuck to the floor. There was also a diaper in the middle of the floor because Lola decided she didn't need to use it anymore, and Hank's bottle was lodged under the ottoman with yesterday's quickly souring milk. Lucy had found a sticker book, and while I changed Hank's diaper in my bedroom, she covered the kitchen window with stickers. The house was a disaster -- or, as I called it during this season, "well-lived-in."

Honestly, I just was working to get through the day. Between breakfast, Tippi Toes phone calls, and what little housework I could get to, I was drained. My first morning thought was *Well, I hope this is what Jessica was wanting.* But as we were about an hour out from Jessica and her team arriving, panic set in. *Oh my goodness, what if this house is way worse than what she was thinking? This is our real life, but what if this is a little bit too much real life?* I started to worry it needed to look only a little "lived-in" so we didn't appear so out of control. You know that feeling before company arrives when you go into beast mode to make your house look perfect, only to act like it looks that way on a regular basis? Yeah, I went there. I set Hank in a bouncer, plopped Lucy and Lola in front of the TV, and busted through my house as fast as possible. I worked up a sweat making my house look like we lived simple, clean, and perfect. And I am sure I yelled at the girls a time or two for not keeping their eyes on the TV or moving a pillow I had already fluffed perfectly on the couch. I was Crazy Mommy on a mission.

After my mad dash cleaning session, I combed the kids' hair, changed them out of their jammies, and hoped we all looked picture perfect in time for the cameras to arrive. Jessica rang the doorbell, and I welcomed her into a beautifully clean house, with a lit candle going and light music playing in the background, as if this was what our normal mornings looked like. On the inside, I was honestly happy I pulled off the vision of a clean house with clean kids, but Jessica was disappointed.

"Oh my gosh, your house doesn't look like mine did when I had littles at home," she said, taking in my home's perfection.

You see, the thing is, she had already made it through this chaotic stage I was currently in. She had *lived* the reality and then was disappointed when what I presented didn't match what she'd remembered.

I smiled. "Oh, I try to keep up daily so it's not a big mess," I said sheepishly.

I know it's really bad to lie, and I bet it is extra horrible to lie when it is your pastor's wife, but I just didn't want my cover blown. Remember, we are trained to show people our polished lives, and that's exactly what I wanted Jessica to see.

"We need this house to look lived-in," Jessica kept saying. "Do you have any toys we could put out?"

Just then, she opened a closet, and from above her head toys spilled out all over the floor. She started clapping.

"This is really good," she said. Then she bent down to Lucy and Lola's eye level. "Can you put your toys all over the room and make it look really messy?"

I laughed. We walked into our kitchen, where you could still see the shine from where I'd mopped. She asked if it was okay if she pulled some dishes out of the dishwasher to put back in the sink and on the counters. *You mean the ones I just put in there that were out from the night before?* I thought to myself. I'd tried to stuff away all the imperfections, and she came over and put things back into the beautiful chaos that was there just an hour before. You see, what she was trying to do at church was film something that was relatable to women, because that would speak to everyone, because we've all been there: a chaotic home, with dirty kids and unbrushed hair, dragon breath from forgetting to brush their teeth, and syrup stains still on their pajamas. What I tried to do unintentionally was ruin her message by making my home look as if it didn't fall into that category, and I tried to make my life seem easier and better than others. It was not accurate and, in fact, was downright fake.

Often, we are so quick to share our beautiful, perfected moments, but the truth is there are a lot of really hard, unpleasant moments stuffed in between that we never want people to see. Why is that? I know for me, I try to hide those uglier moments because society doesn't encourage us to highlight imperfections, and I am scared what people will think about them. The world tells us we should be attracted to polished perfection when, in reality, we relate best to vulnerability. I think I assumed if I shared my snapshots of the hard times, people wouldn't think my family or business was a success. I thought they would only see me as a hot-mess mama and businesswoman. The truth is I probably would have been a lot more relatable to people if they saw the real struggle. And I mean, it is *really* a struggle sometimes, isn't it? But when I think about it, in no way do I wish those tough moments away because I learned and grew so much from those early days of motherhood. I struggled to relax into my messy life, when really I should have been seeing the joy in the short amount of time my babies and my business needed me simultaneously. I look back now with extremely happy memories, knowing that this chapter was just as valuable as the next.

Women feel the pull of motherhood and the pull of building a great family but also find value in doing something we love and making it look like it comes so easy. We justify why we choose what we choose, but that justification is only necessary for ourselves because deep down, we all understand that everyone is going through something. We each wonder if we are doing it right. It's okay, it's normal, but we must be freed of this feeling that someone else has some insight into how to do it better. If we are living in what we feel God and our families have called us to, then we need to be free to be who we are. We are creative and talented, and we also can make a mean bowl of mac and cheese and play on the floor with our kids. The way my house looked during this stage was real life when my kids were one, two, and three. They needed me constantly, and I felt like I could never keep up with the laundry, the sticky floors, the clutter, and all that comes with keeping up with a home. I was the cook, maid, diaper changer, laundry fairy, dish scrubber, and tear wiper. I wanted it to be perfect because that's how I function best, not because I was doing my most important job.

Have you ever wished your life, spouse, kids, or vacations were on the same perceived level as someone else's? Don't get stuck looking at someone else's life wishing it were yours, because God planted us where we are with a purpose. If you choose to use social media, spin your comparison to confetti and allow yourself to encourage, highlight, and celebrate those people in your life. God is a god of confetti. Let your love and words to others be so beautiful that you set an example. Let's radiate the love of Jesus through the words we speak and the confetti we throw! Keep your eyes where you were planted. Don't allow social media or what others appear to be experiencing diminish all that God is doing in your life. *You* are valuable, *your* voice is needed, and *you* are greatly loved. Just as you are.

Take action

Throw confetti instead of criticism

Do you need to lighten up a little on yourself? Or maybe others deserve some grace after you've held the magnifying glass a little too close to their flaws? I have been there. Nagging, worrying, and comparing will not allow us to live the life God has planned for us. We must learn to allow criticism to roll off our shoulders and offer ourselves and others the goodwill we all deserve.

Think about an area in your life where you need to pull out that confetti popper. Who needs your celebration far more than your judgment? My friend, Pastor Bil, has said this line many times: "Get to know me, and I will disappoint you." I love this. None of us is

Jesus, meaning all of us will make mistakes. I may not like the way you coach my kid in sports, or you may not like the choices I feed my kids for dinner, but: grace for both. Humans aren't meant to satisfy each other, only Jesus. If we can come to one another with arms open, grace running deep, knowing we all make mistakes, and instead find the beauty in each other, we will together reflect the body of Christ in a beautiful way. Confetti over criticism, always.

CHAPTER 17

School Was So Hard!

Like, I almost failed.

When I declared my major at the University of Oklahoma, I was unwavering. I wanted to be an elementary education major and, specifically, I wanted to be a fourth grade teacher. At The School of St. Mary, my small Catholic school in Tulsa, I had the most precious fourth-grade teacher, Mrs. Armstrong. I had made up my mind that I wanted to impact others the way she impacted me. I played school with imaginary kids much of my childhood and pictured setting up my classroom, placing an apple on my desk, and pouring into the lives of children in a significant way. That was the desire of my heart.

We've already established how I passed my first year of classes at the University of Oklahoma barely keeping my GPA where it needed to be to get into the school of education. The first semester of my sophomore year, one of my core classes in education was titled CORE CLASS I, and the description read "Elementary Math." I felt confident in this class because addition and subtraction sounded like a breeze for a college student. My first day of class, I descended into the basement of an old building and found room B201. The classroom was filled with mostly women, many of whom were just as excited as I was to become teachers. Our professor had white hair that poofed up about a foot over her head. She carried a colorful briefcase and wore a grimace on her face. There wasn't a warm feeling like we used to have in grade school walking into elementary math; rather, it was a "get straight to work" kind of day. The very first thing that came out of her mouth I remember so well.

"If you think this class will be easy based on the name, think again. Each of you will have to earn a good grade in here, and it will not come easy."

I took her warning like a champion, and I was confidently ready to work. My heart was focused on being a teacher, and nothing would stop me … until it did. Midterm grades were released, and I'd earned a 68%, which is a D. To continue on with the program, each person had to have a grade higher than a 70%. I still had half the semester to go, but the work was getting harder. We did not spend time on addition and subtraction like I had anticipated; rather, we spent time working with numbers in a way I had never learned and struggled to get through. The semester went on, and my grade dipped further. My view of becoming an elementary teacher went from being slightly blocked to completely blocked when my grades came in and four letters appeared: FAIL. I failed the course. The very first class in my declared major was a failure for me. I truly felt the defeat in my soul. I felt really dumb and began to beat myself up. *If you can't pass elementary math, how will you ever teach kids?* I began to believe these negative thoughts about my ability, and I started to get confused about my future.

However, I am nothing if not persistent. I sensed this was the end to one dream, so for inspiration, I combed through the list of other degrees Oklahoma had to offer. Nothing hooked me like the warm thought of being a teacher. To stay in this major, I had two options: I could retake the course with the same grumpy teacher from whom I had a hard time learning the past year, or I could enroll in a three-hour math core at the local junior college down the road that would replace the one at Oklahoma. I opted for the second choice in hopes that the class would be a little easier. Two nights a week, I carpooled 40 minutes with three other students to Oklahoma City Community College and sat through two hours of math. It was dull, it was confusing, but I was passing. It took all I had to put the work in, but my mind was set on teaching fourth grade once I earned my degree. I completed the class with a B and felt confident I had learned the material and should be able to move on.

As I went to enroll in my next year of classes, I saw the words CORE MATH II. My mind was blown. I quickly looked up the classes held at the community college, knowing this was my best option in passing this second math course. My heart sank when I realized my only option was taking CORE MATH II at Oklahoma, and even worse, the same teacher who taught the first class was going to teach the second one as well. I wanted so badly to be a teacher. I didn't understand why it was so hard for me to pass this course. This problem was keeping me from my dreams. The time came that I needed to make a decision: I could either try to conquer CORE MATH II, which I didn't feel confident about, or I could look again at the majors offered and hope I found something that would get me just as excited. I looked, and I looked some more. I read the CORE MATH II curriculum and came to the decision that if I ever wanted to graduate from college, I needed to look at other options for my future.

I pumped myself up, walked to my advisor's office, and officially changed my major to journalism. I enjoyed writing … and that was about the extent of my thinking. I didn't think about a future job; I just had my eyes focused on the immediate goal of graduating college. Switching my major from education to journalism assured me there would be no more math classes. I'd already started Tippi Toes by this point and was busy teaching dance, which is where much of my focus was at the time. (It's anyone's guess why I didn't yet see that Tippi Toes could be a real career for me after college. I think I had the perception I needed an official-sounding college degree for some type of credibility. Rolling my eyes at this younger version of myself while patting myself on the back at how far I've come!)

At the end of junior year, I saw that a summer internship could give me three credit hours toward school. I talked to my parents about the idea, and we connected with a family friend, who got me a job at a Kansas City advertising agency. I was so excited about this opportunity and started to think about what my new future would look like. The summer plan was to work at this advertising agency and earn those three credit hours. I would get to live with my Gram for the summer and experience a new city. I was so excited for this new experience at one of the city's best advertising agencies, but the reality was much different from the vision I had first set in my mind. The company hired a group of ten summer interns, all eager to be assigned our tasks. The first few days were orientation in the office and walking around the building to meet the staff. A few highlights I remember: we got to eat a free lunch on Fridays, received a free parking pass, and, best of all, Blue Bunny was one of their clients, so they kept a freezer stocked with free ice cream. Clearly, as a poor college student who made minimum wage that summer, free stuff was a perk.

My supervisor explained that my job for the entire summer was to sit in a cubicle and thumb through magazines to clip out every advertisement that had to do with fuel. I needed to file them based on fuel type: ethanol, methanol, gasoline, or diesel. I had stacks of magazines piled on my cubicle, which I shared with another intern who talked a lot. My cubicle partner's job was to search the magazines for dog food advertisements. I was strangely envious of him because at least he got the opportunity to look at cute puppies, while all I saw were trucks and fuel tanks. My thumb developed a callus from flipping through so many magazines that summer. I learned way too much about my cubemate, a kid from Peoria, Illinois, and I decided there was no way I was going to work in an office, especially not at an advertising agency.

I couldn't land on why it was so hard for me to figure out my future. I remember a call I made to Adam that summer. He was also experiencing his first internship, with the Round Rock Express, a triple A baseball team.

He loved every minute of it while I couldn't stand walking into work each day.

"You are making more money teaching Tippi Toes fifteen hours a week than you are filing advertising papers in an entire week," he said to me. "You love Tippi Toes. Why don't you take Tippi Toes full-time when you graduate?"

I remember thinking that would be fun, but my head told me I needed a "real" job. My mind was so blocked I couldn't see the beautiful path God had put before me. I was already growing a business right in front of my eyes -- you know, the whole intent of post-college life -- but because it evidently didn't require a college degree, I didn't consider it a realistic option. It wasn't until this conversation with Adam that I put pen to paper. I calculated how many students I needed to teach to equal what a full-time job would give me. As you remember, according to the university, math wasn't my thing -- until it was *totally* my thing, and the numbers clicked. I had 175 dancers dancing with me in the fifteen hours a week I taught as a college student. Each dance student paid $30 per month, which was a $10 increase from when I first started Tippi Toes. In total, I made

$5,250 each month. I knew that coming out of school at the time, I would not make much more than $27,000 a year to start, and my Tippi Toes numbers put me well above that.

One of the beauties of being a young business owner is you don't think of everything. I calculated my monthly amount times twelve months and figured I was going to be rich. I didn't take into account taxes, insurance, payroll, and all the many other expenses that go along with running a business. I had just enough naiveté to not account for any of that important stuff and had full confidence this would work out for me. I was so happy because at this point, my view became clear: I was still able to consider myself the teacher I dreamed of being, but instead of a typical classroom, I'd be in a dance room. Instead of an 8-to-5 job five days a week, I could set my own schedule. As soon as I made this decision, I rushed to the phone to call my advisor, and these were my words to her: "With the hours I have already taken, what degree would get me out of school the fastest?"

I could hear her typing as she searched the school's data. "If you switch your degree to communications, you will graduate in May."

Without another thought, I replied, "Let's make the change."

I was ecstatic. The very thing I was doing the entire time, Tippi Toes, was the very thing God had prepared for my future. In my opinion, God doesn't do this on purpose. I don't think He makes things hard for us to see. I think we do it all on our own. We get so distracted in life. We doubt our dreams, our talents, and our passion. I remember in school so many of my friends had a solid plan. Chanda, for one, went to school to be a physical therapist. She had a road map, knew her timeline, and even had a job lined up when she graduated. I had nothing, or so I thought. I lost sight of what was right in front of me because my plan didn't look like others. There was no road map for me until I drew it myself.

Take action

Overcome obstructions

In the Bible, there are characters throughout that appeared to have a blocked view. David had an affair, Gideon was insecure, Martha was a worrier, Thomas a doubter, Zuccheus was short, Lazarus, well, he was dead, the list goes on and on. As the Bible reads on, they all became overcomers, and the same is true for you and me. When we lean into the places in our life that are hard and uncomfortable and begin to sift through the reasons why and how we can overcome it, we are that much closer to a breakthrough.

- What is blocking your view right now?

- Who do you know or know of that has overcome this similar situation?

- What are you believing to be true about the situation?

CHAPTER 18

Another Learning Experience

If I am still learning, I am still growing.

Embracing Tippi Toes full-time gave me confidence about my life's direction. I planned to start Tippi Toes in Corpus Christi, where Adam and I lived as newlyweds, while still overseeing the Oklahoma and Kansas City operations. One day after teaching a Tippi Toes class, I had a student come up to me with her family and say they were being transferred to a different Navy station and moving to Florida.

Her mom asked, "Do you have any locations in Florida or have any videos we could take with us? Jenna loves Tippi Toes so much, and it would be amazing if we could keep her involved."

Her words stuck with me. She was leaving our city, she loved Tippi Toes, and yet there was no way to have her daughter continue with us. I was sad and frustrated and wanted to find a way to make it work.

As it does, a little idea becomes a big idea, and a big idea takes a long time and a lot of work. I went home and talked to Adam about what had occurred as we both started throwing out ideas on how to expand this business.

"Wouldn't it be really great if we could have dance classes on television and kids could dance from home?" I said.

"That would be so great," Adam agreed. "You could even have little characters that would be engaging to our students, and they would fall in love with them while learning how to dance."

We took action that very night and decided we would write a children's book. Our goal was this book would outline what we hoped would turn into a television show. We wrote a storyline and created four little characters, the most special being Tippi the Turtle. We told how she put on her dance slippers at night and would fall asleep dreaming of being on the stage. We didn't have kids yet, nor were we terribly familiar with children's books. Looking back, it would have been wise to do a little research and learn the best ways to write for children, but nevertheless, we took action. What came out of the effort was something even greater. After a lot of discussion, Adam and I went full steam ahead to put this book through a full animation process.

One of the first things we wanted to do was come up with a theme song for this children's television show. I was excited because after years of teaching dance, we struggled to find music that worked specifically for our classes. There were some great options we already used, but we wanted the music to be fresh and let our dancers' minds know they are full of greatness! What started as a simple conversation with a friend at church turned into a dream project. Joey Davila, our church's worship pastor, was talented musically, but what I didn't know was he could write, perform, and produce music as well. I told him what Adam and I were up to, and I made an "I wish ..." statement about something I didn't think could actually happen.

"I wish you could help us create a Tippi Toes CD, Joey," I said. "Adam and I are dreaming of a children's television show, and to have a theme song that could also be played in class would be so cool."

A few days later, Joey called me. "I don't know why I couldn't create a CD," he said.

I don't know how to read music, I have never written a song, and this entire process was new to me, but that "I wish" statement became a "take action" moment. We met with another creative friend a few times a week to brainstorm what this CD would look like and just decided to take action: my friend and I wrote the lyrics, and Joey worked his magic on the rest of it. We didn't know how it would turn out, we didn't know if people would like it, and we didn't know how to publish it. There were a bunch of things we just didn't know, but we didn't allow that to stop us. *We took action!*

Our theme song "I love Tippi Toes" is still the first song played in every Tippi Toes dance class. The song incorporated the characters we created in our children's book, and it has become a staple for our company. By leaping into unfamiliar waters, I completely changed our classes. Little did we know, taking this action would turn into CD sales, which was another asset to our company. It helped us build upon our brand. Parents supported us and purchased our music. Instead of kids just loving Tippi Toes music while in dance class, they listened to our music at home and during carpool. We saw significant growth in our class registrations after our first CD.

Taking action can mean amazing things if you are brave enough to do it. Our company continues to write music, and each time we see our business grow, our team grows, our support for Tippi Toes grows, and our classes thrive. Our *On Top of the World* CD was one of our biggest CDs ever. It hit both the Kid Albums Billboard chart as well at the iTunes chart, and was submitted for consideration for a Grammy for the Best Children's Album. I think often if that conversation with Joey never moved from the "I wish" to the "take action," where would we be? Would we have grown so much as a company? Would we still be searching for music and never feeling satisfied? This action changed us, challenged us and grew us.

The idea from the beginning was the children's television show, and then came a book, then the music. What we have seen is that the music enhanced the other two projects. We self-published our book, and we put the idea of a television show on hold, but these albums continue to be a driving force for our company.

Take action

Turn your wish into action

Now it's your turn. What is it that you are dreaming for? What is your "I wish" statement? Here, we can do it together:

I wish

_____.

There! You said it, you spoke it into the world. How do we now put action behind those words that are burning in your heart? Let's give it a try by meditating on these questions:

1. How will you feel when you accomplish this goal?

2. What is the first step you need to take to make this happen?

3. Who could you call or talk to to gain more insight on this dream?

4. What will you do this very week to move this dream forward?

TAKE ACTION ON YOUR GOALS

I AM BELIEVING THAT
I will have a best selling book.

TO REACH THIS I WILL
say yes to every opportunity to get my book in peoples' hands and change peoples' lives.

NOW WHAT IS IT FOR YOU?

I AM BELIEVING THAT

TO REACH THIS I WILL

I AM BELIEVING THAT

TO REACH THIS I WILL

I AM BELIEVING THAT

TO REACH THIS I WILL

I AM BELIEVING THAT

TO REACH THIS I WILL

CHAPTER 19

Expanding, and Doing It Our Way

Have you guys ever thought of franchising?

When we started thinking about expanding Tippi Toes, we thought the best way was to get Tippi the Turtle on television. Shoot for the stars, right? We outlined a TV show, a children's book, and had just created a theme song. Adam and I jumped a plane to California to meet my sister Megan and her husband Chris, as well as my cousin Kerry and our friend Reid (the same one Adam worked for in Texas), who were both mentoring us at the time. The plan was to meet animators we had been talking with over the phone and through email and put a plan together to pitch our idea to networks. The animators had done some work with shows currently on TV, so we felt like we had a great shot of making this happen.

We piled into the rental car and drove to what we thought was their office. Have you ever had someone pitch you only to realize his or her pitch was far better than the product? Well, that was the case this day. We walked into what turned out to be their home, and my eyes were drawn to the troll trinkets that lined their windows, one after the next, thousands of trolls. Susan and Joe greeted us, and this was the first time we had ever laid eyes on them. She wore what appeared to be a bathrobe post-shower, and he quietly towered over me with long white hair tucked behind his ears. Joe's button-up shirt and cargo shorts made me believe he was more eager to surf than land our deal. If first impressions were what sealed the deal, this deal could have been considered dead because of their unprofessionalism. They escorted us to their kitchen, and we sat at their table to discuss how to move forward. We quickly realized who they said they were and who they really were didn't match. Our ideas didn't sync with theirs, our budget didn't line up with what they were charging, and the entire meeting felt clunky. We left their house feeling 100% defeated.

Adam, Megan, Chris, Kerry, Reid, and I went back to our hotel to regroup. In my mind, I thought it was the end of this dream. I was embarrassed we had made such an effort and spent so much money to make this meeting happen.

As we sat throwing out ideas around a lobby table, Reid said something that sparked a huge new phase for our company: "Have you guys ever thought of franchising?"

We all looked at each other. I started to halfway grin and said, "No, I have never, ever even thought of that."

He explained how he thought it could look and that we could reach a lot more people by opening franchises. This also solved the problem we had about obscurity and not having the funds to produce a TV show with the right people. Potentially, if we could grow our Tippi Toes audience and make money franchising while we did that, a TV show could be a reality down the road. The idea intrigued us, and we couldn't shake it. Megan and I didn't waste any time: we flew back home and began researching.

Sometimes you just get lucky in life, and this was one of those moments. Megan called a big franchising company to ask how we could get started. They transferred her several times before finally connecting with a man who explained that yes, she had reached a franchising company, but they didn't accept clients unless they already had twenty franchises. The funny thing about this, in my opinion, is that once a company has twenty franchises, why would you need help? It's most challenging in the very beginning stage. But as Megan continued talking with the man on the phone, he took a liking to her -- how could you not? – and he decided to help us out.

"I should not do this," he said, "but I will give you a man's name who just retired, and I think he will be very helpful to you."

Megan quickly called this retiree and explained our hopes and needs with Tippi Toes. He explained how he had been working so many hours for so long and wanted to live a retired life, but he really liked our idea. Megan felt good about the conversation, so she set up a time for us to meet him. We decided it was worth it to explore what was there and what could possibly be in the future.

Three weeks later, Megan landed in Austin, Texas, and Adam and I drove up from Corpus Christi to pick her up from the airport. We all drove the hour and a half to meet at his favorite place to eat in Waco, Cafe Cappuccino. We wanted to know if Tippi Toes could be franchised, and, if so, how that would look. As we were introduced to the man Megan spoke with on the phone, we saw right away that he was smart, kind, and knowledgeable in the franchising business after being in it for many years. He had binders filled with an extensive look at our business. The work he'd already invested in us motivated us to move forward. Our new consultant was willing to help and had the kindest heart. He explained how he was burnt out on the big franchise companies and he'd decided we were the perfect transition for him into his retirement. With a firm handshake, followed by hugs all around, we were ready to go.

Time and time again throughout the Bible, God places people in the right place at the right time to be used by Him, and we really felt like God gave us this man at the right time to help us take Tippi Toes to the next level. At the time we were wanting to franchise, the big franchise companies not only wanted us to already have twenty franchises before they would talk to us, but they also wanted us to have a large down payment. That company would get up to 40% of our sales and royalties of the business. I am thankful we didn't have the upfront money because if we had said yes to the big franchising company, we would have been stuck in a horrible contract. Our consultant listened to where we were, understood where we wanted to go, and based his price on what we had at the moment. As we grew in business, only then would his payments grow as well. He treated us more like a team and a family than a business transaction -- the same approach I take now with our Tippi Toes owners. Starting out with this kind of relationship made it easier to take action from the start so we could also be smart with our money.

After the first year working with this consultant, we were ready to sell a franchise. Our first Tippi Toes franchise sold in 2008 to Andrea and Tom Dangel in Cincinnati, Ohio. We spent the next year with Andrea, teaching her, learning from her, fine-tuning the areas we needed to clarify for her, and adjusting so when the next family purchased a franchise, it would flow even smoother. The second year of franchising, we sold to five additional families. Our goal with each sale was to make sure the new owners believed in our company's mission and vision, wanted to make a community impact, and were willing to work as hard as possible.

Franchising became a huge part of Tippi Toes. We have 35 franchise locations in the United States and one master franchise operating in China. Now women around the world can open a business with the support of Tippi Toes corporate, collaborate with other like-minded women, and be part of a sisterhood that often feels more like family than business. The way we have grown Tippi Toes has become more special than anything I could have ever imagined.

I really feel like one of the biggest tragedies in life is that far too many people go to their grave with a suitcase full of dreams they were too scared to unpack. They never took action. Yes, there will be hard stuff that happens along your journey, but that is the good stuff, too. Sometimes God doesn't immediately improve a difficult situation because He is working on changing your heart or your perspective. With challenges can come beautiful blessings. When I was fired from my waitressing job, I discovered my potential of starting Tippi Toes. When I was cut from the dance team in high school, I went on to become a state tennis champion that same year. When the idea of a children's television show fell short, franchising blessed me even more. The hard can be hard to overcome, but seeing the beauty that follows is always worth it.

Take action

Don't let heartbreak mean defeat

Leaving that meeting in California, our bodies oozed with defeat, but that feeling we left with turned into purpose after our core group's fruitful conversation. Just because the TV show wasn't going to work yet didn't mean we were sunk. In fact, it meant quite the opposite: it meant we would be adding people to our team in this mega, new venture, and with some smart new franchise owners, we could move forward faster.

Franchising has been pivotal to who Tippi Toes can reach. The sisterhood and growth our franchise owners have had has allowed Tippi Toes to reach places we never would have alone, through this built-in support and camaraderie. Believe me when I say the heartbreak you have experienced in life isn't a loss. In fact, many times you can find good and purpose in the feeling of defeat. The soreness in our hearts can cause us to quit or ignite us to find a way to move forward with purpose. It's so easy to know the proper thing to do after something has happened -- hindsight, am I right? -- but so hard to predict the future.

Looking back at some of your disappointments, what have you pushed on to do? How did you access bravery from a place of despair, and can you just take a minute to recognize the power in your having done so? You are so strong, friend. You're still alive, despite pain. You're still dreaming, despite rejection. You've forged ahead when lost or alone a million times over, and you can do it again now and then the next time, too. The more heartbreak we have, the more prepared we are to navigate it in the future. I won't ask you to be grateful for those heartbreaks, but I will ask that you see them for what they are: gained knowledge. You are smarter now for having survived. Onward.

CHAPTER 20

Know When to Take Action

Sometimes what feels like a loss is actually a gain.

Let's get back to *Shark Tank*, can we? I told you about how Adam boldly signed Megan and me up to be part of the show. After making it several rounds through the rigorous tryouts and sending in paperwork, video answers, and pitching to producers over the phone, we were in! What I haven't shared yet is how it all played out behind the scenes.

We landed in Los Angeles ready to pitch our idea of Tippi Toes DVDs kids could watch (back when that was cool); however, there was a lot of work needing to be done before the cameras rolled. We wanted kids to perform on camera with us. I mean, the "sharks" can't seem as scary if we have kids with us, right? Due to the laws of TV, we had to hire professional kids. *What?* Well, neither Megan nor I had ever held a casting call before, so we winged it -- my specialty. We found a website where we could post the job we needed done with the date and location of our auditions. We rented a small spot at a hotel, and floods of parents and their little darlings showed up. Megan and I walked the room, greeting everyone and smiling at all the adorable faces. I am sure this was a far cry from what they had experienced in other auditions, but what can I say? Southern hospitality runs deep.

Group by group, we called kids back to a room to have them follow along with us dancing to "I Love Tippi Toes." This was the most fun and hardest job we had while in LA. We needed three kids, and we had our choice of more than one hundred. We made notes. We were looking specifically for children who were extremely well behaved and could follow along with us well. We had one shot in the shark tank and couldn't afford for a little one to get scared, throw a fit, or not be ready to perform. We were looking for kids with a big stage presence and a huge smile. It was so much harder than we thought, because remember, these were "professional kids."

Finally, after three hours of auditioning the children, we had selected our three. They were told to be ready for us to call them at a moment's notice and meet us at the Sony lot where filming would take place. We arrived on a Sunday and had been told we could be there anywhere from one to seven days. We just were waiting for that phone to ring in our hotel room each morning. When it didn't ring by 9 a.m., we knew we weren't selected for that day. It wasn't a guarantee for us to even *get* a phone call, so each day we woke up waiting and hoping. When the call didn't come, we had the day to ourselves to, yes, practice our pitch yet again, but also explore LA. We rented a smart car to get us around town and drove it shopping, around Beverly Hills, and through neighborhoods of the rich and famous. Even with all the fun we were having, getting into that shark tank was still all we could talk about.

On the last day, day seven, our phone finally rang. We gave a sigh of relief when we heard the news: *this is your day.* We were told to meet at 11 a.m. in the lobby for a white van to pick us up. Giddy, Megan and I chatted nonstop. Maybe it was the nerves, the excitement, or the fact we had been waiting for this very moment for months. As we were dropped off outside Sony Pictures Studios in Culver City, California, we spotted the sharks on break. We had officially arrived. We waved and smiled, but they were all business and walked straight past us. We were escorted to our green room and asked to wait inside the room for instructions. Soon, a young woman working as an intern knocked on our green room door as Megan and I were patiently waiting. "Hair and makeup are ready for you," she said. *Pinch me now! We are in LA on the Sony lot being told hair and makeup are ready for us.* All we could do was smile big and chatter to the ladies in charge of our primping. Next it was time to get mic'd up and wait for the shark in front of us to complete his pitch.

There we stood, palms sweating and hearts pounding in excitement. We knew it wasn't a guarantee that even if we did pitch we would be picked to be aired, but we were hopeful. Music played, doors slowly opened, and Megan and I -- along with our professional kids -- walked down the long hall with sharks swimming on either side. All we could do was smile. Our Tippi Toes music started, and all five of us started dancing. A glimpse of what our classes looked like back home. We had a display of our characters Tippi the Turtle, Buzz the Bee, Bopa the Butterfly, and Freddy the Frog adorning the room while our DVDs were neatly placed on the table.

After our dancing and saying goodbye to the kids, we dove in, with not a second to waste. "Hi Sharks," we said. And just like that, we were in business. Not skipping a beat, we had spent months memorizing our pitch, and it came off perfectly. (Thank you, Megan, for pushing us to practice). The questions started firing back at us from shark after shark, but we were armed and ready for anything to come our way. When you own your own business and create the processes, it is hard to be stumped, because we had made it all up anyway. The sharks salivated over our franchises and weren't as much interested in our DVDs. They loved that our program could be duplicated around the country and we had smart businesswomen running it.

If you are familiar with *Shark Tank*, you know Kevin O'Leary, also known as Mr. Wonderful. He offered us a deal -- a deal we would never take, but a deal indeed, and I actually really liked him. Then Barbara Corcoran came in with an offer, asking if she could have more of the company than what we originally offered. Next, Mark Cuban chimed in with a proposal. He told us he didn't want to compete with the other sharks; he wanted us to come to *him* with an offer. If he liked it, he'd take it. If he didn't, then we could listen to the other sharks. We fired back: $100,000 for a 30% stake in our company. Mark jumped up, clapped his hands, and headed over to us for a hug. The deal was done. Or was it?

Megan and I flew back to our homes excited about the deal we had just made. Our real work started over the next few months, dissecting the contract Mark sent to us. We hired a lawyer to help us understand the lawyer jargon. The more he would explain, the more my heart would begin to nudge me, whispering, *This isn't the direction*. Call after call, we continued to try to make it work. We *wanted* it to work. My heart was heavy, and so was Megan's. If we signed this contract, so much of what we loved would be taken away. We are a family first company, and signing the dotted line would pull me away from my family and have me flying all across the country to get more franchise owners; volume was important to Mark's strategy. I love our community of women and how it feels more like family than a business, and it was clear that would have been taken away. We did all the things to make the best decision we could. While many people thought we should just sign and be done, our lawyer and my pastor said the opposite. Adam and I went into Pastor Bil's office, as he was one of the few who knew the situation we were in. "I don't think it is in your best interest," he said plainly. He confirmed what I already knew in my heart.

I called Megan, and she said, "Bear, I feel the same way." So I took the time to write Mark a heartfelt email telling him we would not be signing the contract. Yes, we turned down a billionaire telling him we didn't want his money. It was a tough email to write. We worried if it was the right decision. I hit send, and then I prayed. I was very specific with God: "God please make it clear we did the right thing."

Fifteen seconds later, I heard a ding and opened an email from Mark. His response: *That is a bullshit response sarah in every way shape and form. I hope this is not how you treat your future partners. M*

Thank you, God, for this email. Thank you for the reassurance that we did the right thing. This response showed me the type of partner we would have been dealing with. And with that, the deal was dead.

Sometimes in business and in life, we get that instinct, that nudge from God to move in another direction. Having discernment to actually move takes courage. It isn't always easy, but I am always thankful when I do listen and act.

Tippi Toes is no stranger to heartache, and this happened with someone we were incredibly close to. For several years, we really enjoyed working with the consultant who had helped us franchise. The work was productive, and we accomplished a lot together. But over the span of a year, we'd been struggling to get on the same page with him. He had opted to work less as he moved closer to retirement and was less available to us. He'd scaled back to working just a few days a week, and the work he was doing wasn't to our satisfaction. We were working more and getting busier, much of which he questioned, yet there was some occasional friction. This relationship just wasn't beneficial any longer. Megan and I talked for months to come up with a solution, and honestly, the only thing left on the table was to take action: it was time for us to move on from him so we could keep guiding Tippi Toes into the direction we had dreamed. We never entered this collaboration thinking of an exit plan -- I tend not to approach life that way -- so when it is time to think of an exit plan, it's painful. Throughout the whole process, our goal was to make sure he knew he was loved and how thankful we were to have him working with Tippi Toes. We wanted to honor him for that service, but also let him know we were struggling with finding common ground. We wanted to express that our dreams were being snuffed out before we could fully express them. We simply had to take action.

One Friday in May, Megan and I sat on the phone with him discussing items we thought weren't highly important or very productive issues, and I just felt a premonition in my gut. This was the time. Megan and I had already discussed what needed to be said. We even put a timeline together to begin a few months from this day on how we were going to enter this uncomfortable conversation, but, friends, the door opened and there it was. I got a clear nudge, and so I mustered up my courage. I began to tell him how great he was and how thankful we were to have him be part of our Tippi Toes team. I shared with him the vision we had to move things in a different direction and the many reasons why this current relationship wasn't working any more.

Gosh, you guys. It stung at first. It was not fun at all. From our side when it came out, it stung and then on his side when he received it, it stung even more. Then, we started talking about how much we had accomplished together and how fun it had been to witness and celebrate the company's growth together. In true form, he gave us a few reasons why he thought our new direction was a really bad idea, but then he laughed.

"Well, I think you two are ready for this," he said. "This is what I've prepared you to do for the last eight years. Let's put a plan together, and I want to watch you fly."

Once everything was said and out on the table, I realized he had been waiting for us to make this move. Through his guidance, he wanted us to be the ones to actually take charge. You see, taking action sometimes surprises you on the other side. I was so worried about hurting his feelings while he, on the other side, was grooming us for the next step. Our consultant will always be a special part of Tippi Toes and will continue to help with some unique projects, but now he can enjoy retired life and we can move at a much faster pace. He can watch all these seeds he planted blossom.

You can know what you want, surround yourself with good people, be good every day, and find out what's blocking your view, but if you don't take action, then you're still stuck in the same spot. If you really want something and believe it's worthy of your headspace and time, you will find a way. If you don't fully believe in what you are doing, you will find every single excuse to not take any action. (In a way, your action vs inaction is telling: if you make no movement toward a dream, then maybe it isn't really your dream anymore after all. As they say, you aren't a writer if you aren't writing.)

What does "take action" mean to you? Does it mean being brave enough to speak up at work when you have an idea you believe in? Does it mean starting that business you've long dreamed of? Does it mean buckling down and disciplining your kids the first time, even though it stings a little to do so? In all areas of life, to make advancements, you *must* move from one comfortable -- and sometimes uncomfortable -- spot to another through initiative and effort. Rarely are relationships or ideas grown when standing still.

***

One day, a few summers ago, Adam took action: he booked a flight and spoiled me rotten. This "take action" was the best kind, in my opinion. For me, there is nothing more fun than being surprised. I find that it's very difficult to surprise me, because I feel like I'm always anticipating and expecting the next move. As a mom and a business owner, to keep my family and business on track, I have our schedules planned, meetings set, and a firm hold on what our day to day looks like. Not much interrupts my day that I don't see coming. Well, all of that proved untrue in June of 2017. I was doing some unglamorous work around my house, putting the folded laundry away in my closet, when I got a text from my handsome husband.

"Do we have plans June 3rd-6th?" I read in the text message.

"It looks clear," I wrote back. "Is someone coming to town?" We tend to have lots of visitors in the summer months, and I started thinking about Procailo and Alexa bringing their boys for a visit like we have talked about for so long with our old friends.

"No, just wondering," he replied.

"Do you want to go someplace or do something, or just relax at home?" I pressed him.

"I want to take you someplace," he said.

And he had plans for that very weekend to take me somewhere special. There was a catch, though: he wouldn't tell me where we were going. Instead, each day leading up to the surprise, he offered a clue. The clues included simple words: bikini, sheep, pig, grand cookie, flip, flop, and belly. I was so confused. Then, to make sure I wouldn't find out the destination, which he was confident would get leaked to me, he lied to our kids, our extended family, and our neighbors, telling them each different destinations. He did not want this big present to be revealed.

"Is this going to be in the United States?" I questioned.

"Yes," he said confidently. "I don't have our passports."

Then I asked another question. "Are we going to Vegas?"

He just smiled. I figured I had it nailed. Adam can't normally keep a secret. He gets this half grin on his face and looks away when he isn't being fully honest. I figured by the look he gave me, I'd guessed right and he was trying to keep up the lie.

The day for our trip arrived. We met Adam's dad at a gas station halfway between where we would fly from. His parents offered to hang out with the kids for the weekend. Adam and I started our vacation with a night together in Nashville, since he said we had an early flight the next day. We had an awesome dinner at a Brazilian steakhouse just off Broadway in downtown. Then we strolled up and down the street, peering in at the honky-tonks, listening to the music pouring out of them, and checking out all the sights of downtown Nashville. With our early wake-up call, we headed back to the hotel before it got too late. I was so excited to head to Las Vegas -- or so I thought.

Our alarm rang out at 4:30 the next morning, and we headed to the airport. It was pitch black, and although it was early, we were both talkative and excited for the day. Adam didn't allow me to check in online or go anywhere near the counter to check in our bags; he took action when we arrived, since he thought I still didn't know where we were headed. All of a sudden, as only Adam and Sarah can travel, the airline attendant slapped "Late Check-In" baggage tags on our luggage, and there we were, racing through the airport. I have no idea how we got so late, but the attendant told Adam to run. He still wouldn't give me my boarding tickets as we raced to the gate, passing the sign that said where we were going: Fort Lauderdale, Florida. I was so confused. I didn't think I could be surprised, but the fact that we weren't going to Vegas really threw me for a loop. Adam just smiled, and I didn't get to say another word to him, because we were separated on the plane since we arrived late.

Sitting on my own during the flight, I started researching things to do in Fort Lauderdale. We'd been there long ago to visit his grandfather, so I knew it would be a fun weekend. Possibly he had planned for us to do some of the things we did on our last trip, like tour the Everglades and drive to Key West. Then the weather forecast made my heart sink: rain, rain, rain, rain. Four days straight of solid rain. I felt bad for Adam. He had planned this great getaway, and it was going to rain the entire time. Poor Adam.

When we landed after our two-hour flight, we got off the plane, and I hugged him so tight. I told Adam I thought Fort Lauderdale was such a great idea and I never would have thought to go here.

"Well, we're not there yet," Adam said. "We still have one more place to go. Let's grab our bags and head out of the airport."

We all know the big TSA airport rules. You can't leave the terminal and then easily go back in, so I figured we had to be driving somewhere. Hand in hand, we walked toward the exit. About halfway down the hallway, Adam stopped and I caught him staring at the monitors. We had already completed our flight. What was he searching for? Then he looked at me.

"Let's take another flight," he suggested.

My jaw dropped. Grab another flight? I couldn't believe he wasn't finished surprising me. "Adam, what on earth?" I said. "What are we doing? I'm so excited!"

"Well, we're leaving at 11:15," he hinted.

I ran over to the screen to see which planes headed out at 11:15. Zero planes. There were zero flights leaving at 11:15. *Huh?*

Adam reminded me of the clues he gave me the week before. "What sound does a sheep make?" he asked.

I made the sound baaa, and I started laughing. "We are going to Baaa?"

"What kind of meat does a pig produce?" he asked.

"Hot dogs?" I guessed. "Pork chops? Ham?"

"Yeah, ham!" he said.

"So ... Baaa Ham? Baaa Ham? We're going to Baaa Ham?" I was still so confused.

Then he reminded me about the Grand Cookie clue. "Who makes those vanilla sandwich cookies?" he said.

"Grandma's cookies?"

"Yep, Ma!" he stated. "Baaa Ham Ma."

"Oh, my. Bahamas! Baaa-hamas! We're going to the Bahamas?" I screamed and cheered.

We boarded our next flight, which was a quick 45 minutes in the air. As the plane descended, all I could see was blue-green water and lush green trees. You could see right down to the shaded areas where rocks and seaweed lay underwater. The air was hot when we landed, and the sun shone brightly. No sign of rain in the Bahamas. Once we collected our bags, I sat and enjoyed the smell of the island and wind in my hair while Adam arranged a taxi.

There's this part of the airport that is lined up with room after room of all-inclusive resort information booths, or at least that is what I thought it was. Adam and I had been to an all-inclusive with some friends a few years ago, and it was fabulous. Since you pay for everything ahead of time, you aren't fussing with a purse, counting out a tip, or trying to budget, because that is all taken care of ahead of time. Adam waved me over, and we walked up to one that said Sandals, a couples resort in several tropical places around the globe. Since it isn't our travel style to stay in these, I assumed Adam was asking for directions from the man at the front desk. He gave our name, and I looked at my husband in disbelief. Sure enough, Adam Nuse booked an all-inclusive resort for us in the Bahamas. I was floored. Maybe, just maybe, I *can* be surprised.

As I reflected on our trip, I thought about a few things. First, Adam totally took action. There are so many scenarios that could have happened instead: we could have stayed home, we could have decided together where to go, but being surprised is the most wonderful gift ever. This took work on Adam's part, planning, booking, and asking his parents to help with our kids for the entire four days. He prioritized me over all the other millions of things he had to do. He took action in making me feel special, making the experience fun, and allowing me to relax and enjoy.

I also thought about how the key to any great relationship is taking action with your most precious asset: your time. There have been times in our marriage when we get sideways and either our kids or jobs require more of our time than what we're able to give each other. When this happens, it is key for Adam and me to take action by communicating and stepping back to reprioritize. When communication breaks down, the other person feels unloved and unaccepted. When we put others first, we make God's word alive and active by living out "love your neighbor as yourself." For me, I know when I spend time in God's word, time in prayer asking God to be the master of my life and for direction in my day, my day quickly lines up by what's important. When I pray to God asking Him to use me as a vessel and push me in the direction He wants me to go, I feel more confident in the dreams that are in my heart. When I feel most connected with God, I know that He will bless me when I take action and dream big. When I think of Jesus first, my frustrations with others lessen and I have more grace toward those in my life. I don't get it right all the time, and, to be fair, get it wrong more than I do get it right. I allow my days to become busy, my mind to become stressed, and my goals become about me more than shining a light on my partner.

When I first met Adam, we were in college. He had just come back from a summer of working at a Christian sports camp. He was on fire for Jesus, and I had extreme curiosity. He asked me on a date, or so I thought, yet instead drove me to a campus praise and worship night. I had never experienced Jesus in this way before. A room of college students madly in love with Jesus and singing at the top of their lungs. I looked at Adam. His eyes were closed, his hands were raised, and he was singing. It is a picture I have in my mind still today, and it was in that moment he began to lead me into a relationship with Jesus that radically changed my life.

My husband has a calm spirit that fully relies on God in any situation. In fact, the first verse he taught me when we met was Proverbs 3:5-6: "Trust in the Lord with all your heart and lean not on your own understanding but in all ways acknowledge Him and He will direct your path straight." Ever since that day, Adam points me and our family to this verse. It is so comforting to have him lead in a way that is biblical and God-honoring. Early in our marriage, when we were trying to define who we were as a couple, we struggled with communicating and managing our time together. As we worked through this, we learned a lot about ourselves. For me, I love to just share my entire heart, my hurts, my victories, and go deep. I want to sit, hold hands, and work out anything that I feel is happening between us right then and there. Adam was the complete opposite. He didn't share at all or communicate anything to me -- or that's at least how I felt. If something would bother him, he would seal up tight like a clam. The more he did this, the more I talked to fill in the quiet space. We have learned an incredible tool that we use in our marriage, with our kids, and in our business relationships: we start our conversation with "*The story I am telling myself is....*" When we do this and finish the sentence with the thoughts in our mind, we are able to share with the other person where our feelings are and all the thoughts swirling in our head. Former professional hockey player and coach Wayne Gretzky once said, "Most players skate to where the puck is. I skate to where it is going to be." If we can apply this to taking action in all of our relationships, we can be proactive on what is to come. We know that if our marriage is strong and healthy, our kids will feel secure and thrive. If our marriage is healthy, we'll be more efficient at work. If we are at our best, even when it requires some extra effort, then together we can handle more.

We're often so busy trying to move up the career ladder that we miss out on taking action with people around us. Let's not forget to invest in all the areas that are most valuable to us and invest in those people and spaces. I think God enjoys watching us take action. He is ready to pour blessings on us, but I think he loves to see us come part of the way on our own, too. Taking action can be a simple text or a phone call to a loved one, maybe it's randomly sending balloons or flowers, and maybe it is a note in the mail or an early morning donut delivery. What can you do? How can you take thoughtful initiative to show you care?

Have you ever looked in the driver's side of the car next to you to find them texting at the wheel? If you're completely honest, you might even admit to honking at them while your own phone is in your hand. Stay in your own lane. Keep your eyes on your own paper. Run your own race. It's all the same: to find your own greatness, stop looking at what you see on social media and playing the comparison game. Stop checking LinkedIn to find the latest, greatest job someone just posted about. Stop comparing your husband, wife, kids, vacation, city, home, friends, food, job, schedule, family, and life to what others have. Friends, keep your eyes on your own life and focus on your unique gifts from the heavenly realm and do something *extraordinary* with your time here on Earth. Fall in love with your husband. Fall in love with your kids. Take care of your plot of land. I promise you will see a harvest.

For me, extraordinary is to impact the kingdom of God by using my gifts. I want to live into my potential with limitless abundance. In order to find that greatness in your own life, you must choose to be good every, single day and take action. I believe in you, I am cheering you on, and I know God created you uniquely. You, my friend, are destined for greatness!

Acknowledgements

Jeez, I have thought a lot about this section of my book. How can I possibly acknowledge everyone who helped make this book possible? There are so many people who have helped shape me, many of whom you will read about in the pages of this book.

Thank you Jesus for allowing me to dream big, for giving me gifts that I can use to glorify your kingdom, for allowing me to share your name, and most importantly for changing my life completely. My heart's desire is that when people read my story, they see you, they are drawn to grow closer to you, and they appreciate the gifts you've given them to run their race. I am completely in love with you.

Adam Nuse, you are my hero. Without you, there is no point in dreaming big. You make it all worthwhile. You push me to dream bigger, ask me to dig deeper, and constantly are pointing me to live the life God called me to live. I love this life we have built together, and I am thankful you regularly encourage and support every single crazy idea. I am proud of you. I am thankful you are an amazing dad to our kids and love me like crazy. Jackpot husband. Thank you.

Lucy, Lola, and Hank, how did I get so lucky? You are the kindest, bravest, most loyal friends. You share Jesus in fun and unique ways, and you constantly push me to aim high. You support me, encourage me, write notes to me, love me, and show me that I can do all things. I pray more than anything this book impacts you, your children, grandchildren, and our family for generations to come. It is because of you three that I want to keep aiming higher. There is nothing you can't do, so run hard the race God has set before you. Impact the world for Jesus!

Mom, Dad: really, me, a writer? You knew it; I didn't. You believed in me when I didn't. You supported me when I felt like I couldn't do more. There has never been a moment you downplayed my dreams, ever since I was a little girl. You never allowed a moment to pass without teaching me how to grow. Thank you for pouring into me, for your wisdom, for your prayers over my life and my future. I hope when I grow up, I am just like you both.

J-Bird, look at us now: one hour apart with family and work now colliding. How did we get so lucky? You are a constant source of strength for me, and I love that I know I can always count on you. You cheer me on, support me, believe in me, and laugh with me. Thank you for believing in my wild ideas and joining the Tippi Toes family. I learn so much from you about life and friendship. I adore you.

Megs, where would I be without you? My girl who dreams alongside me, believing really anything is possible. God is good, and He knew this wild ride would be more fun next to each other as friends, moms, and business partners. All the lessons we have learned in business and life, so many have been side by side. There is nobody I would rather learn with than you. I believe this is just the middle of our story, with so much more to come. Keep dreaming big. You inspire me daily. I am cheering you on in all you do!

Emily, Courtney, Katie, and Alaina, it was you four who said yes to helping me develop and think through how I could tell my story best. You were patient with me as I would fumble, and you believed in me. Your belief kept me going when I would doubt myself. Emily, remember my first manuscript? Can we even call it that? You helped shake out so many ideas and got my story making sense. Sitting across the table from one another at Starbucks, I would try to convey what my heart wanted to tell. Courtney, a pure WENIUS = word + genius. You have a way with words and storytelling, and your gift allowed my story to come alive even more. You kept with me as we would sit and think of the perfect word to replace another -- brain surgery in a different kind of way, like you used to say. I will never forget when you simply said, "We need more adjectives." You were right. I cherish our time sitting across from one another at my desk in deep conversation -- and our occasional dance parties when you would help me craft the perfect sentence. Katie, you helped me reach the finish line. I wasn't sure how I would finish this book and say, "Yes, here is the final copy," but you did it, and you didn't stop. Thank you for seeing me through to the end. You are talented, creative, and an editor in every sense of the word. Alaina, our email exchanges had me tossing my brain into your inbox, and you always caught my ideas in your open arms. You grasped my vision, and then you spent time making it flow with my stories and my intention so our dear readers could see more clearly.

You have a gift, and I am so thankful your creations are the visuals of this book. You each have helped shape me as a writer and -- dare I say? -- author now. Thank you. I hope you are each proud of what you did. You helped me. I couldn't have this book in my hands without you.

My precious Tippi Toes sisters and family. What a journey we have been on together. It was you who allowed me to grow, learn, and lead. When I didn't know what I was doing, you offered grace and allowed me to fumble. You have challenged me to think outside the box and cheer me on with my crazy ideas. Without you, there are no Tippi Toes classes. You impact the lives of children in your communities and help them to be seen, loved, and heard. You are the heroes of this story. Thank you! And all of our amazing Tippi Toes teachers, families, and students, thank you for choosing Tippi Toes and for supporting our program. I am forever thankful for each one of you.

Miss Shelly, it was you who instilled a love of dance in me when I was a little girl. To this day, you cheer me on in whatever I am doing. You have always slowed down to talk with me and cared what was going on in my world. Thank you for speaking life into my life. All the conversations, compliments, and smiles I have stored up in my mind, and you have been a source of so much of my inspiration. As a little girl, I wanted to be just like you, and I am thankful you were that role model for me.

Joey, look at where our music has come. You are the best teammate, and I am so thankful all those years ago you said, "I know this is going to be big." Because of you, little children all around the world dance to positive, encouraging, upbeat songs that shape their life. You did that. Thank you for sharing your creativity and pouring so much into our Tippi Toes music. You are a gift to us, and your fingerprints are all over this company.

Caroline, Chanda, Brooke and Sarah Frances you may be characters in this book to the reader, but you are so much more to me. You have shaped me. You have inspired me and played pivotal roles in my life. Thank you for your friendship, your love, and for all the stories and laughter. Little did any of us know, there would be a book written about all of our shenanigans. I adore you so much! Never forget how special you are to me.

Bob, it was you who saw this book in me long before any words were typed. The way you said it made me believe I could do anything. I watch you and am inspired by the way you encourage, love others, and shine Jesus. You are an inspiration to so many people, and I am thankful for your impact in my life. Tatave and Haley, girls, you include me and have opened your ams to me as I have tried to navigate this book. Bob is lucky to have you as part of his team. You are difference makers!

Noel and everyone at World Help, thank you for living a life that inspires the rest of us. Thank you for living with such conviction that you will not stop until people's lives are saved and changed. Your organization has shown me the darkest parts of our world, and I'm convinced that with action, there can be hope. I am so proud to know you and want to help in any way I can.

Pastor Bil and Jessica, when Adam and I were newlyweds, our lives changed when we found your church. You have inspired us, led us, taught us, loved us, and cheered us on. You have been incredible mentors to us in marriage, parenting, and business. I love the way you love Jesus and His church. We are with you to work to "take as many people to heaven before we die, period."

To you, the reader, thank you for picking up this book. I pray it inspires you to live a life full of purpose. You are created unique and authentic, and the world needs your voice, talent, and love.

Made in the USA
Columbia, SC
22 September 2020